COUNTDOWN TO GLORY

A Commentary on the Book of Revelation

LES WHEELDON

Copyright © 2019 Leslie John Wheeldon

All rights reserved.

ISBN: 9781079761634

All scripture quotations unless otherwise indicated are taken with thanks and appreciation from the World English Bible (public domain).

Scripture citations marked 'NKJV' are taken from the New King James Version®. Copyright © 1982 by Thomas Nelson. Used by permission. All rights reserved.

Cover photo by Sharon 607238 unsplash.com

DEDICATION

This book is dedicated to the Suffering Church and all who are enduring tribulation for their faith in Jesus Christ.

ACKNOWLEDGMENTS

I was encouraged to write this book by my dear friend Oleg Fedeorev after teaching this subject in the Bible School of Omsk in Siberia. I thank him for his persistent encouragement.

Special thanks are due to Graham Cline for many enjoyable hours spent together reviewing the manuscript and discussing the subject.

Robert G. Betts has been a constant friend and helper in this project, combining deep scholarship with fervent love for the Lord.

Thanks to Mary Seaton for her careful reading of the manuscript and many helpful emendations.

With gratitude to my loving and dedicated wife Vicki, for her constant encouragement to fulfill my calling from the Lord.

Table of Contents

Clearing our minds		1
Chapter 1	The Greatest Revelation of Christ in the Bible	8
Chapter 2	Ephesus, Smyrna, Pergamos and Thyatira	18
Chapter 3	Sardis, Philadelphia and Laodicea	35
Chapter 4	The Clearest Vision of Heaven in the Bible	44
Chapter 5	The Lamb Opens the Scroll	49
Chapter 6	The Countdown begins	53
Chapter 7	The Multitudes of the Redeemed	61
Chapter 8	The 7th seal: God's judgments	69
Chapter 9	The 5th Trumpet: A Flood of Demons	75
Chapter 10	John's calling is renewed	81
Chapter 11	The Church at the Close of the Age	87
Chapter 12	God's triumphant people	101
Chapter 13	The Beast and the False Prophet	110
Chapter 14	The Blessedness of the Redeemed	121
Chapter 15	The 7 Angels and the 7 Last Plagues	128
Chapter 16	The 7 Vials of God's wrath	131
Chapter 17	Babylon	136
Chapter 18	The Fall of Babylon	147
Chapter 19	The Coming of Christ	153
Chapter 20	The Millennium and the Last Judgment	158
Chapter 21	The New Jerusalem	166
Chapter 22	The New Creation	172
Study Guide		179
Appendix 1	Methods of studying Revelation	188
Appendix 2	Tribes of Israel	193
Bibliography		195
Index		196

CLEARING OUR MINDS.

All through the centuries since Jesus Christ established His church, believers have drawn great comfort and blessing from reading the book of Revelation. Through periods of persecution, Antichrists, and world-shaking events, the longing of His people is echoed in the words *"Amen! Yes, come, Lord Jesus."* (Revelation 22:20).

We may feel daunted by the study of such a challenging book. But God will bless each one of us who comes with a mind that is open for Him to speak to us. We need to allow the words to search our hearts and prepare us for times ahead. In approaching the interpretation of the book of Revelation, the primary intention of this book is to present a simple and straightforward account of its meaning. The main aim is to allow the chapters to speak to us as individuals; to challenge us in our walk with the Lord and our readiness for His return. God desires to comfort His people with the sure promise that this world with all its troubles will soon pass away and a new world will take its place.

The Mystery of the Book.

The mystery of Revelation is that it is written in such a way that believers in every age can draw help and comfort from its pages. This explains why all believers have thought they were living in the last days, from Paul, through Luther, Wesley and right down to present day expositors. The point is that we are not to be troubled by current events but to study the book and gain the comfort of the message of Revelation. This message is as follows:

- God is in control. The focus of the book is not on troubling current events but on the fact that God is on His throne. The universe is not a battle ground between two equal forces. God alone is sovereign and ruling behind the scenes.
- Christians are called to overcome the Antichrist culture of their generation. They are to be separate from the spirit of the world (Babylon) and pursue love and holiness (see also 1 Corinthians 2:12 and 2 Corinthians 6:17).
- Christ is coming. There may be suffering, tribulation and pain in this life, but there is hope of another world. We are to 'gird up our loins' and run the race in joyful hope of the Resurrection of the dead and the rapture[1] of the saints.
- This world is passing away. The physical world we see is temporary and will be replaced by a new creation after the return of Christ.

Matching events in Revelation, with Events Past, Present and Future.

So, in setting out to allow the book to speak to our hearts it is vital to realise that there are some verses in Revelation that can be identified as specific events in the course of world history whether past present or future. What are these events?

- The cross. In Revelation 5:6 John saw the Lamb that had been slain ascending to the throne of God. This is the central focal point of all history and John described it from heaven's point of view.
- The end of the age, marked by the rapture of the saints and the return of Christ. This will be at the last trumpet which is described in Revelation 11:15. It is also described in Revelation 19:11-21.
- The Day of Judgment: Revelation 20:11.

---

[1] The word "rapture" does not occur in English translations of the Bible. It is derived from the Latin "rapturo." This word means to be caught up and is used in the Latin New Testament of 1 Thessalonians 4:17. "Deinde nos qui vivimus qui relinquimur simul **rapiemur** cum illis in nubibus." (Vulgate) "Then we who are alive *and* remain **shall be caught up** together with them in the clouds." (NKJV) The English word rapture means "bliss" and it is used to indicate the act of being caught up with the Lord in the air at His return.

The quest to try and relate current events with Revelation is extraordinarily difficult and many who have tried have had to admit their error. Martin Luther, William Tyndale and many other reformers were persuaded that the pope was the Antichrist. John Wesley believed that the Antichrist was the Ottoman Empire. Many have believed that Communist Russia fitted this description. Some who lived through the Second World War believed that Hitler fitted the bill and that events in the 1940s were leading to the end of the world and the return of Christ. In post war years, the return of Israel to nationhood in the middle-east gave rise to expectation that Christ would return before the year 2000.

None of these speculations was completely wrong and that is precisely the point. It is not the purpose of the book to help us correlate the verses of Revelation with specific people or events. Rather it is the purpose of the book to give us an understanding of principles that underlie the events unfolding in our day. Once we realise this we cease worrying about whether we can perfectly fit in things we read in our newspapers with the final countdown to the return of Christ. The book of Revelation will give us keys that help us to identify Antichrist rulers and philosophies in every age. The apostle Peter saw clearly that Rome was Babylon (1 Peter 5.13). This does not mean that only Rome was and is Babylon. Today our whole civilisation has the spirit of Babylon described in Revelation 17 and 18.

In addition to this, every few years there are big cosmic events that produce a frenzy of speculation including:

- The millennium bug (remember that?)
- The dramatic alignment of all the planets that would place stress on the earth's core and produce a season of terrible earthquakes in 1987
- The four blood moons in September 2015.

Many readers will not have noticed these 'cosmic events' and some who heard of them will have quickly forgotten them. It is vital that we are not easily or "soon shaken or troubled in mind" (2 Thessalonians 2:2) by the things we read in newspapers.

Overview of the Messages of Revelation

The book of Revelation has a message intended to reach the hearts of God's people.
It has many distinct sections, which are not all primarily targeted at explaining the return of Christ. Of course some sections are exclusively about future events.

- Chapter 1 describes the greatest vision of the risen ascended Christ given to any person in all of history.
- Chapters 2 and 3 are searing prophecies directly from the lips of Christ given to sift and purify believers.
- Chapters 1 and 10 describe the way God prepared John to be a prophet to the nations.
- Chapters 4 and 5 are the clearest description of heaven in the whole Bible.
- Chapters 6 -11 describe the timeline of world history from the cross to the return of Christ.
- Chapters 12 -19 describe the main players in world history, including Israel, the church, the Antichrist dictators and philosophies, and finally Babylon.
- Chapters 20 -22 describe the events after the return of Christ and the new world that will replace this one.

From this brief overview it will be seen that the first five chapters have little teaching on the second coming but are messages for the church in every age. The last three chapters are about the events that will unfold after the return of Christ. It is only the 14 chapters from 6 through to 19 that direct the reader to the events that will culminate in the second coming of Christ.

Revelation: a call to worship!

There are many great scenes of worship in the book of Revelation and many awesome songs are described. This is because the message of the book is that God reigns in majesty and power. He will reign through all eternity and He will conquer all evil.

Jehoshaphat put his singers in the forefront of the battle (2 Chronicles 20:21). This is the great background of the book. While men build their armies and unite to practise evil, believers will sing and glorify God.

The Pitfalls to Avoid.

"Though St. John the Evangelist saw many strange monsters in his vision, he saw no creature so wild as one of his own commentators." G.K. Chesterton.[2]

The words of Chesterton make us smile, but why is it that so many books and speakers turn us off? Here are a few pitfalls to avoid:

1. Obsession with the sensational. Our interpretation may be so unreal that when prophecy is fulfilled we may miss it. For example we may overlook the Great Tribulation afflicting the church in history and around the world today. It is interesting to reflect how the fulfilment of Messianic prophecies of Christ were missed by so many rabbis who had invested their lives in studying the signs of His first coming.
2. Embracing details of interpretation rather than the main message. Will there be a chip implant needed to conduct business? Will a 3rd temple be built in Jerusalem? These things may or may not happen. But the main message of the book is a call to prayer, holiness and worship; and an assurance that we have a God who holds the future in His hands.
3. Assumption of infallibility. Not all commentators are right so why should we assume that our interpretation is 100% correct? Once more it is vital to realise that the message of repentance to the churches of Asia is clear and unambiguous, while the identity of Antichrist is obscure.
4. Beware of charts that seek to harmonise every detail of the book. Revelation is written in such a way that Bible students can see many different patterns or applications. Even if we cannot fit everything in, or understand every symbol, the main message is clear: look at Christ, stay close to Him, for we are His bride eagerly awaiting His return.
5. It is a mistake to apply this book to the future alone. It has a message that helps every reader in every age understand their world. It also has a message that keeps every believer burning brightly with love for the Lord

---

[2] G.K. Chesterton, *Orthodoxy* p. 29, New York: John Lane, 1909.

The Purpose of this Book.

The true purpose of this book is to deepen our walk with Jesus Christ and to stir us to 'watch and not sleep' as the Countdown to Glory unfolds.

"Watch therefore, for you do not know when the master of the house is coming - in the evening, at midnight, at the crowing of the rooster, or in the morning- lest, coming suddenly, he find you sleeping. And what I say to you, I say to all: Watch!" (Mark 13:35-37)

God promised He would send His son to die on a cross for the sins of the world. He also promised He would send the Holy Spirit to apply this cleansing power and recreate human beings from the inside by the gift of a new heart. Both of these prophecies have been fulfilled to the letter. God has also promised that His son will come a second time, not to suffer but to rule.

To watch is to persistently and patiently live in the light of the coming of Christ for it is as sure and certain as the sunrise. This fact is to shape our thinking. We will then be empowered to live in the most profound freedom from the influence of the world. The world with all its burdens and cares often seems so permanent and strong but it is passing away, and it is as we realise this that it loses its grip.

The coming of the Holy Spirit is the down payment, the first instalment and taste of Christ's everlasting kingdom. Now we are to live keeping short accounts, without grudges, without baggage, ready to leave at a moment's notice and stand before the Master. This prophecy is not in one or two obscure verses but is the main subject of the book of Revelation. It is the subject of His teaching when He sat with His disciples on the Mount of Olives. It is the framework that undergirded all His teaching from the parable of the wheat and the tares to the parable of the wise and foolish virgins.

The command of Jesus Christ to watch is a solemn charge to all His followers to firmly establish this truth as the framework of our thinking and living. This will remove any fear about the future and produce a joyful anticipation of the glory that is about to sweep across this world.

On 19th May 1780 in Connecticut USA, a dense fog combined with dust to produce an unusual darkness that the inhabitants had never witnessed before. One hour the sun was shining, the next everything was plunged into the darkness of night at midday making it impossible to read. The Connecticut State Council was in session and members were convinced it was the Day of Judgment, and requested an adjournment so they could go home and get ready to meet their Maker. One member, Abraham Davenport objected: "I am against an adjournment. The day of judgment is either approaching, or it is not. If it is not, there is no cause of an adjournment; if it is, I wish to be found doing my duty. I wish therefore that candles may be brought."

*

In the early part of the 20th century a farmer from the mid-western United States was leafing through a magazine and saw an ad for a barometer. He filled in the form and sent it off with his payment. A week later it arrived. He eagerly unwrapped it and admired the beautiful instrument with brass fittings and a beautiful dial. Then he noticed that the needle was stuck pointing at the word "hurricane." He tapped it and fiddled with the instrument to no avail. With a sad heart he wrote a letter of complaint and wrapped the device in neat brown paper. He had just finished writing the return address when the hurricane struck….

*

CHAPTER 1

THE GREATEST REVELATION OF CHRIST IN THE BIBLE.

The Context: John on Patmos.

Revelation 1:1 *This is the Revelation of Jesus Christ, which God gave him to show to his servants the things which must happen soon, which he sent and made known (literally "made known by signs") by his angel to his servant, John,* **²** *who testified to God's word, and of the testimony of Jesus Christ, about everything that he saw.*
³ *Blessed is he who reads and those who hear the words of the prophecy, and keep the things that are written in it, for the time is at hand.*
⁴ *John, to the seven assemblies that are in Asia: Grace to you and peace, from God, who is and who was and who is to come; and from the seven Spirits who are before his throne;* **⁵** *and from Jesus Christ, the faithful witness, the firstborn of the dead, and the ruler of the kings of the earth. To him who loves us, and washed us from our sins by his blood;* **⁶** *and he made us to be a Kingdom, priests to his God and Father; to him be the glory and the dominion forever and ever. Amen.*
⁷ *Behold, he is coming with the clouds, and every eye will see him, including those who pierced him. All the tribes of the earth will mourn over him. Even so, Amen.*
⁸ *"I am the Alpha and the Omega," says the Lord God, "who is and who was and who is to come, the Almighty."*

⁹I John, your brother and partner with you in oppression (tribulation), Kingdom, and perseverance in Christ Jesus, was on the isle that is called Patmos because of God's Word and the testimony of Jesus Christ.

The apostle John was exiled around 95 AD to Patmos off the coast of eastern Turkey during the persecution under the Roman Emperor Domitian. This was the second wave of persecution by the Roman government against the first century church in which approximately 40,000 were martyred. The first was from 64-67 AD under Nero and the third was in 98 AD under Trajan. Evidence suggests that John wrote the book while the prophecies were being given to him (in chapter 10 John mentions that he was about to write something but was stopped by the angel). God was sending a word of comfort through John to His suffering people. John was an old man, perhaps around 85 years old (if he had been 20 when called by Jesus beside the Sea of Galilee in Matthew 4:21). The style of the Greek is rough and that of the fisherman. Despite his great age he was imprisoned in a labour camp, possibly even working in the stone quarries that were on the island.

The phrase "signified" in verse one indicates that it was put in sign or symbolical language. John was given a series of visions and prophecies which would be understandable only to God's people. The book is an open secret and the symbols are not hard to find and are in plain sight within the rest of the Bible. These symbols are to be found preeminently:

- In the book of Genesis which recounts the origin of all things, as Revelation in turn describes the end of all things.

- In the books of Ezekiel, Daniel and Zechariah which describe events around the end of the world.

Chapter One

Slain by the Magnificent Vision of Christ

[10] *I was in the Spirit on the Lord's day, and I heard behind me a loud voice, like a trumpet* [11] *saying, " What you see, write in a book and send to the seven assemblies : to Ephesus, Smyrna, Pergamum, Thyatira, Sardis, Philadelphia, and to Laodicea."*
[12] *I turned to see the voice that spoke with me. Having turned, I saw seven golden lamp stands.* [13] *And among the lamp stands was one like a son of man, clothed with a robe reaching down to his feet, and with a golden sash around his chest.* [14] *His head and his hair were white as white wool, like snow. His eyes were like a flame of fire.* [15] *His feet were like burnished brass, as if it had been refined in a furnace. His voice was like the voice of many waters.* [16] *He had seven stars in his right hand. Out of his mouth proceeded a sharp two-edged sword. His face was like the sun shining at its brightest.* [17] *When I saw him, I fell at his feet like a dead man.*
He laid his right hand on me, saying, "Don't be afraid. I am the first and the last, [18] *and the Living one. I was dead, and behold, I am alive forever more. Amen. I have the keys of Death and of Hades.* [19] *Write therefore the things which you have seen, and the things which are, and the things which will happen hereafter;* [20] *the mystery of the seven stars which you saw in my right hand, and the seven golden lamp stands. The seven stars are the angels of the seven assemblies. The seven lamp stands are seven assemblies.*

John mentions that it was the "Lord's day." This might be the first day of the week, a Sunday when the Lord's people were in the habit of meeting (Acts 20:7). This does not mean that it was John's day off from the rigours of his exile! There are no details of how and where the vision was given. It may have been in the night hours after an exhausting day.

However it is also possible that the Lord's day was in fact the one day of the year that was dedicated by the Romans to the worship of Caesar.

Domitian had inaugurated a day for this purpose and used the very same phrase.[3] Loyal Roman citizens were content to declare that "Caesar is Lord" on this day and offer incense to his image. But Christians and Jews refused this act since they regarded it as a denial of their faith. Jews were given exemption from this practice and Christians too were exempt for a while since they were initially regarded as a Jewish sect. However by the end of the first century Christians were denied the right to abstain and this was a major cause of fierce waves of persecution.[4] If this is the meaning of the phrase then the book of Revelation was a comfort to the believers suffering for their faith on this very day. One of the central purposes of this book is to impart the tremendous strength and encouragement flowing from heaven to uphold believers passing through tribulations.

The phrase "in the Spirit" refers to a conscious awareness of being in the presence of God, in the dimension of the Spirit. It does not mean he was in a trance, but was consciously passing into the awareness of the King and His Kingdom. If a person is never conscious of being in the Spirit then their inner faculties are still unawakened. Being "in the Spirit" is a foundational blessing of New Testament Christianity. Without it, believers will become dry and merely intellectual. This does not mean they will be dull and boring. They may be lively and interesting but they will be lacking the ability to minister the knowledge of God through the Spirit. It is in the Spirit that we are conscious of God and it is through the Spirit alone that we know God. Every believer has this privilege, to live in this present world, and to be conscious of heaven and things unseen. John was consciously aware of God's presence when suddenly a voice spoke. By this voice John was suddenly ushered into a unique experience that would complete the Bible: the self-disclosure of God and His rule over the human race.

The voice of Jesus resounded like a trumpet and John turned to see the

---

[3] "The Lord's day" - "ἐν τῇ Κυριακῇ ἡμέρᾳ".
[4] David Pawson, *When Jesus Returns,* Hodder & Stoughton 1995, p 110.

voice. The vision that He saw was the glorified Christ. God's method of changing human lives is always to reveal His Son. Sinners like Levi were converted after a few seconds in His presence (Luke 5:27-28). Paul the Pharisee was a fierce enemy of Christ and was turned around by a glimpse of Christ (Acts 9:4). Paul later identified the revelation of Christ as the means by which Christians are to grow spiritually:

> *"But we all, with unveiled face seeing the glory of the Lord as in a mirror, are transformed into the same image from glory to glory, even as from the Lord, the Spirit.." (2 Corinthians 3:18).*

It is remarkable that although John had walked with Christ for some 60 years, when he saw Him unveiled he fell at His feet as dead. The glory of God is revealed to our hearts in ever increasing depths. When we think we have understood, then God opens another window to glimpse a little more and we fall once more as dead at His feet. Death is so obviously a negative force in our normal experience, but dying in the presence of Jesus is the sweetest place of release that we can ever know. Death in His presence is not the death of positive things, but the death of all that is negative. There, our selfish ambitions, our unbelief, our fretting and our hardness all die. The result is that we are His, supremely and totally His. We are free from using Him to our advantage and most of all free from self-consciousness into transforming God-consciousness.

As John lay in the dust at the feet of Jesus he felt a hand touching Him, raising him up, and removing his fears. The glorified Christ was bending down to comfort his messenger with a touch of love. A Revelation of Jesus is transforming and allows the love of God to reach the deepest parts of our being. John was not only slain, he was raised to deeper friendship and companionship with the matchless Son of God.

This event was the preparation of John as a prophet to bear the message of Revelation without the bias of his personality. This is the way that God prepares all His ministers, purging them from their personal leanings to minister the pure word of God. Chapters 2 and 3 are words given by Christ for the seven churches that John was familiar with. He lived in Ephesus, and had probably ministered in all the other 6 churches. He now saw and heard things from the mouth of Jesus that He had probably never imagined. He was ready to communicate the specific prophecies to the churches and the wider visions concerning the return of Christ.

The Greatest Revelation of Christ in the Whole Bible.

What John saw and described in these verses is the greatest Revelation of Christ anywhere in the Bible. It is vital to grasp this fact and to ponder the significance of this vision. The chapter as a whole reveals 16 things about Jesus:

1. Jesus is called the Son of Man (v 13) which is His title 84 times in the New Testament. 21 times this title is mentioned in respect to His second coming as Judge of all the earth. This is the most arresting part of this description since it emphasises His incarnation as a human being. The Hebrew New Testament translates this Greek phrase as "The Son of Adam." The implications of this title are immense and indicate that the vision is of the glorified humanity of Christ and hence the destiny of all believers. Believers will never be divine, but we are to be so infused with the presence of God so that we are transformed into His image.

   "Beloved, now we are children of God, and it is not yet revealed what we will be. But we know that, when he is revealed, we will be like him; for we will see him just as he is." (1 John 3:2)

   The believer is to be a partaker of the glory that is to be revealed in Christ (1 Peter 5:1). There are aspects of Christ that are unique to Him, aspects that relate to His divinity and it is impossible for our weakened minds to grasp the full significance of God's plan revealed in Christ:

Chapter One

"For whom he foreknew, he also predestined to be conformed to the image of his Son, that he might be the firstborn among many brothers. Whom he predestined, those he also called. Whom he called, those he also justified. Whom he justified, those he also glorified." (Romans 8:29-30)

2. He is the Alpha and Omega (v 11) the first and the last, the beginning and the ending, having the first word and the last on every soul and situation and nation.

3. His feet are in a furnace (v 15) – indicating stability combined with passion. This also indicates that He is standing on the altar that burns constantly before God. Christ has a being that is inseparable from the cross. He lives in a constant offering of Himself to God the Father in love. The fire also speaks of His burning purity (Hebrews 12:29).

4. His hair is white like wool (v 14) – indicating purity and wisdom.

5. His eyes like flames of fire (v 14) – searching, all seeing. To stand before that fearsome gaze is to be laid bare, with no place to hide.

6. Standing in the midst of the churches (v 13) – the High Priest attending the eternal flame of the seven lamps. The priests in the tabernacle would keep the seven-branched Menorah constantly burning. Jesus is in the midst of His church, trimming the hearts of his people to burn steady and bright with constant love. This gives us an understanding of the role of the church; that we are to be gathered around Him to receive His ministry to us, and for us to minister in turn to Him.

7. Clothed to the feet (v 13) – indicating a robe of solemn dignity and majesty. It is also the priestly robe that He wears as our great High Priest.

8. Girdle of gold (v 13) – this belt symbolises righteousness and faithfulness: *"Righteousness will be the belt of his waist and faithfulness the belt of his waist." (Isaiah 11:5)*

9. His face was as the sun (v 16) – radiating the glory of God. This was also how He was revealed on the mountain of transfiguration (Matthew 17:2). The sun pulsates with waves of light but Christ emanates spiritual waves of transforming holiness that pierce the hearts of all who gaze on Him, changing us into that same holiness.

10. The sword in His mouth (v 16) – the power of the truth spoken by Him, penetrating, converting, transforming. Christ speaks with knowledge that is supernatural and penetrating to the depths of who we are. He also speaks with a voice that is laden with power to transform those who hear.

11. His voice is as the sound of many waters (v 15) – indicating both grandeur and variety. The waters that flow from His being are powerful, abundant and magnificent as of a great waterfall like Niagara, but they are also varied, from the tinkling brook in the high mountains, to the quiet rippling of the great broad rivers of the plains.

12. Holding the seven stars (v 16 and 20) – indicating His intimate authority over His messengers. Jesus holds His ministers in His right hand. These are described as angels but the Greek word indicates messengers in general and it is unlikely to refer to angelic beings since it is improbable that God would communicate with angels through an apostle. These stars are almost always the leaders and ministers of the churches, but in some churches the people walking closest with God may not be the recognised leaders of the churches.

13. Holding the keys of death and hell (v 18) – the prize of Calvary; all power and authority are now given to Him. It should be of supreme comfort to all believers that Jesus alone decides the day of our

death, and Jesus alone decides the eternal destiny of human beings. Medieval tradition often portrayed Satan as ruling hell, but the Bible reveals that God rules over all by His Son and His holy angels (Revelation 14:10).

14. He bears the name of Jehovah (v 8) – the Being One "He who was, is and ever shall be" the timeless unchanging One. Jesus Christ is the ever living, ever existing God.[5]

15. His testimony (v 18) – the One who was dead and is now alive for evermore. Jesus is Himself the greatest witness of the things that He accomplished on the cross. This is also the testimony of His followers who fellowship with Him in the power of the cross. They have taken up their cross and died to self.

16. He is the ruler of the Kings of the earth (v 5) – He is king over all. When a new President of the United States sits in the Oval Office of the White House, there are reverberations as he begins to use the levers of power. Jesus, the love of God incarnate, is seated at the right hand of God over all the thrones of earth and He decides who rules the nations. He rules and is able to overrule any decision by any man. Christ obtained His rule through suffering and humility, rejecting the shortcut of bowing to Satan (Matthew 4:8-10).

It is vital to linger in Revelation chapter one as it is one of the most important chapters of the Bible and the key to the book of Revelation. It is Jesus Christ who is to fill our consciousness as we consider the difficult days through which we pass on our life's journey. The subsequent chapters describe many dark phases in world history and the greatest comfort is to know that Jesus is the dominant figure over all.

---

[5] The Greek word "ὁ ὤν" literally means "The One who has being" and is the phrase in the Greek Septuagint that translates "I am" in Exodus 3:14.

The power of the revelation of Jesus Christ is that it leads to transformation. Chapter 1 is a beacon of light and hope that illuminates the course of world events. We must return to this chapter over and over again to bathe in the light of the infinite supremacy and majesty of Jesus Christ.

CHAPTER 2

EPHESUS, SMYRNA, PERGAMOS AND THYATIRA

In chapters two and three Jesus dictated to John His messages to the seven churches of Asia. The word "Asia" is misleading for this is not referring to the huge continent of Asia but to a small Roman province in what is today, south west Turkey. The chief city of this region was Ephesus and it was through the ministry of Paul that this whole region heard the gospel:

> *"This continued for two years, so that all those who lived in Asia heard the word of the Lord Jesus, both Jews and Greeks."*
> *(Acts 19:10)*

It can be assumed that all these seven churches came into existence in the time of Paul's extended stay in Ephesus from AD 53-57. John wrote the Revelation some 40 years later so these churches were no longer in the freshness of their beginnings. John probably travelled around these seven churches and was therefore well known among them.

These seven churches are representative of the various kinds of Christian assemblies at any given time in history. Some have suggested that they are symbolic, each representing an era of church history (Ephesus being the church of the 1st century which left its first love and Laodicea the church of the $20^{th}/21^{st}$ century which is lukewarm). This interpretation does not adequately address the differing conditions of the church in different nations. It is rather that these seven kinds of churches are to be found at any one time in church history, both in the 1st and the 21st centuries.

These letters address all the main issues that can afflict churches, from immorality to the challenges of persecution, from outstanding success to a complete loss of perspective. Any church leader reading these letters will find prophetic insight into their situation and the keys to unlocking a deeper move of God in their locality.

The Number 7.

This number is in the very fabric of the book of Revelation. It indicates completeness or perfection. Here are the main occurrences:

7 churches

7 Spirits of God

4 x 7 = 28 times the Lamb is mentioned

7 Seals

7 Trumpets

7 songs of worship:
1. The worship of the Creator Rev 4:8-11.
2. The worship of the Redeemer Rev 5:8-14.
3. The song of the multitude from the Tribulation Rev 7:9-12.
4. The song of the 24 elders Rev 11:16-18.
5. The new song of the Redeemed Rev 14:1-3.
6. The song of Moses and the Lamb Rev 15:3-4.
7. The song of the marriage of the Lamb Rev 19:1-8

7 Blessings in the whole book which are for:
1. "He who reads and he who hears." Rev 1:3
2. "They who die in the Lord." Rev 14.13
3. "He who watches." Rev 16:15
4. "They who are bidden to the marriage supper." Rev 19:9
5. "He who has part in the first Resurrection." Rev 20:6
6. "He who keeps the words of this book." Rev 22:7
7. "They who wash their robes." Rev 22:14

Chapter Two

The number 7 is found elsewhere in obvious places such as the 7 days of Creation, the seven days of a week, the cycle of 7 years with the seventh year a Sabbath year of rest culminating in the year of Jubilee marking seven cycles of seven (Leviticus 25:1-9).

The number 7 is also found in less obvious places such as the first Hebrew sentence of the Bible which has seven words. It is also found in the 7 churches of the New Testament epistles – 1. Rome, 2. Corinth, 3. Galatia, 4. Ephesus, 5. Philippi, 6. Colossae, 7. Thessalonica.

The number seven assures us of God's perfect plan and order in His working in the human race. Just as the universe is filled with perfect design, (from the double helix of DNA to the orbits of the planets in our solar system) so too there is order and design in the unfolding of the ages. We are not victims of the random flow of history. We are to discover the great plan of the Creator, the Redeemer and the benevolent ruler of the universe. There is a great plan to bless the human race, and the more we walk with God, the more we see His craftsmanship, designing the flow of human history as a whole, and our own lives in particular. This message of a plan that is being outworked is one of the main teachings of the book of Revelation and is intended to impart peace to the believing reader, as we realise that God already knows the end of all things from the beginning.

Ephesus – the Loveless Church

***Revelation 2:1** "To the angel of the assembly in Ephesus write: "He who holds the seven stars in his right hand, he who walks among the seven golden lamp stands says these things: [2] "I know your works, and your toil and perseverance, and that you can't tolerate evil men, and have tested those who call themselves apostles, and they are not, and found them false. [3] You have perseverance and have endured for my name's sake, and have not grown weary. [4] But I have this against you, that you left your first love. [5] Remember therefore from where you have fallen, and repent and do the first works; or else I am coming to you swiftly, and will move your lamp stand out of its place, unless you repent. [6] But this you* *have, that you hate the works of the Nicolaitans, which I also hate. ⁷ He who has an ear, let him hear what the Spirit says to the assemblies. To him who overcomes I will give to eat from the tree of life, which is in the Paradise of my God."*

Ephesus was the largest city of the Roman province of Asia. It was the site of one of the Seven Wonders of the Ancient World: a huge statue to the goddess Diana. Paul's preaching, from around 53-56 AD, had so broken the idolatry of Diana that there had been a riot by the traders in religious artefacts (Acts 19:25-27). No one was buying them anymore.

From its beginning, the church at Ephesus had been given the privilege of receiving the greatest ministry; having been founded by Paul, pastored by Timothy and then having John the beloved apostle in its eldership and perhaps even Mary the mother of Jesus in its membership (imagine having tea with Mary and John the apostle and hearing all the fascinating stories they must have known). The church had been born in a great revival. Among the early assemblies it was one of the most advantaged and most successful churches. Yet it is important to recognise that not all that impresses man, pleases God. The church was hard-working and had resisted false apostles. Both Paul and Peter prophesied that false teachers would multiply in the last days: 2 Timothy 3:1-9 and 2 Peter 2:1. This meant that the church had a great pride in its authenticity. They had kept the "truth" in its doctrinal purity. Moreover the church had not given in to weariness and fainting.

How sober then was the warning that even this great church had lost its spiritual compass. Jesus spoke[6] and said that the church had fallen and thus indicated that as far as He was concerned, the condition of this church was dangerously similar though not identical to other fallen beings: "How you are fallen from heaven, Lucifer son of the morning,"

---

[6] Jesus spoke and introduced His comments with the phrase "these things says" which is the Greek "Τάδε λέγει." This is the phrase used in the Septuaguint "thus says the Lord" introducing the words of God Himself.

Chapter Two

(Isaiah 14:12). Many Bible teachers also speak of the fall of Adam, although the phrase is never used in the Bible. This church had slipped and fallen from its exalted position.

The lesson is that success always brings with it the danger of smug self-satisfaction and pride which is the greatest sin of all. We are blessed because God is good and gracious to sinners, not because we are so great and worthy of blessing. Jesus warned His followers that "the last will be first, and the first last." (Matthew 20:16). This indicates the temptation to pass from the desperate need of grace of the new convert, to the self-righteous moral high ground of the Pharisee.

The church was continuing in the form of a successful church but was heading for disaster. They had abandoned their love for the Lord and for each other. They had not "lost" their first love like a misplaced purse, they had "forsaken"[7] it, turned their back on it. Duty was now their motive, not love. Outwardly, all was the same, but inwardly there was a coldness and distance from Christ and from each other. The times of prayer would have been marked with great prayers of biblical precision but coldness of heart. The teaching would have been marked with great accuracy but no passion. The worship would have been a shadow of former days when zeal and love moved them to great acts of renunciation. Acts 19:19 tells of the burning of books worth 50 thousand pieces of silver (approximately 3 million US dollars).

If one had challenged the believers on this issue they would probably deny that they had abandoned the way of love. It is the prophetic word of Christ that reveals the deliberateness of their departure from the ways of God. It is so easy to focus on doctrinal purity over loving behaviour. These two prongs of the Christian life are not necessarily in conflict, but the danger of focusing on correctness is that it may mask a deep lack in the vital area of agape love. The believers in Ephesus had

---

[7] "You have left your first love" verse 4. The Greek word for "leave" is "aphiemi" meaning to leave, forsake, neglect.

chosen the path of excellence in every spiritual dimension except that of love.

There are many attractive alternatives to love including religion, good works, personal happiness, etc. Now the church at Ephesus had chosen the path of mere duty and was cold and close to death. Though this may seem hard to believe, Paul teaches in 1 Corinthians 13:1-3 that the greatest sacrifices, knowledge, spiritual gifts and even faith are meaningless and empty if there is no love.

The answer for this church was to return to first love and to seek God for a renewal of intimacy in prayer and devotion. When love has ceased to rule a church, whether it has been lost through neglect or abandoned by deliberate choices, then the only way for such a church to proceed is to begin again to cultivate the inner life of love and worship for Jesus. Love is a fruit of God's presence through the Spirit, not a product of the human will. It is to be cultivated like a tender plant that will bear fruit in due season. Jesus commanded the church to repent, to confess their pride and their coldness. Unless there is a deep change of heart love cannot take hold and flourish. Hebrews tells us that we are to repent of dead works:

> *"Therefore leaving the teaching of the first principles of Christ, let us press on to perfection—not laying again a foundation of repentance from dead works, of faith toward God."*
> *(Hebrews 6:1)*

> *"How much more will the blood of Christ, who through the eternal Spirit offered himself without defect to God, cleanse your conscience from dead works to serve the living God?"*
> *(Hebrews 9:14)*

The Ephesian believers were to repent not of immorality but of the dead, loveless, religious practices that were so foreign to the heart of God. This was not the worship of idols carved in wood and stone, it was the worship of a golden calf of doctrine (Exodus 32).

Sound teaching is vital:
> *"Pay attention to yourself, and to your teaching. Continue in these things, for in doing this you will save both yourself and those who hear you." (1 Timothy 4:16)*

But it must not replace the love of God which is of paramount importance. The believers were commanded "to repent and do the first works." The first works include a return to the beginnings of every move of God, in an outpouring of the Holy Spirit, cleansing and making the love of God real in the lives of God's people. Believers were to begin to practice love, by caring for the weak, visiting the sick, feeding the hungry and clothing the poor (Matthew 25:35-36). They are not to wait for feelings of love but are to do deeds of kindness while praying for the fragrant blossom and fruits of love to flourish in their hearts.

Jesus warned the church that if they did not repent He would remove their lampstand from its place.[8] It is noteworthy that John saw seven oil lamps standing independently. Each local church stands in its own right and can be removed by Jesus whenever He decrees. What this warning meant is not explained. It could be that Jesus would remove all power and favour, leaving the church with a lifeless empty shell that would decline till it disappeared. What is certain is that Christianity was swept from Turkey in the coming centuries and that today there are only small pockets remaining. F.W. Farrar visited the ruins of Ephesus in the 19th century and wrote:

---

[8] The King James translation "candlestick" is inaccurate and the word refers to a lamp fed by oil. The Greek word is "luchnia" and is the word used in the Greek Septuagint in Exodus 25:31 for a "menorah." Both the Greek and Hebrew words refer to an oil lamp but neither refers exclusively to a seven branched lamp. It is possible that John saw seven Menorahs each with seven branches, but since it is not specified it is of no vital significance. (Solomon had 10 menorah made for his temple, 1 Kings 7:49). It is clear however that John saw 7 lampstands not one with seven branches.

> *"Its candlestick has been for centuries removed out of his place; the squalid Mohammedan village which is nearest to its site does not count one Christian in its insignificant population; its temple is a mass of shapeless ruins; its harbor is a reedy pool; the bittern booms amid its pestilent and stagnant marshes; and malaria and oblivion reign supreme over the place where the wealth of ancient civilisation gathered around the scenes of its grossest superstitions and its most degraded sins"* (Farrar, "Life and Work of Paul," ii., 43, 44)

It would be wrong to rush past these first chapters, since to do so would be to miss the meaning of the whole book. Unless this initial prophecy is understood, the rest of the book will be irrelevant.

Who were the "Nicolaitans?" The answer is not recorded anywhere, but the Greek word means "overcomer of the laity" (literally "overcomer of the people") suggesting the formation of a spiritual elite that set themselves apart from the average Christian. Whether or not this is the doctrine of the Nicolaitans, Jesus said He hated this teaching and He certainly hated the exclusivity and spiritual snobbery of the Pharisees. Elitism rears its head again and again, with special forms of hierarchy or clergy who are the privileged few. Elitism is against the character, teaching and Spirit of Christ.

The final word to the church at Ephesus was a promise that those who overcame would eat of the tree of life in the midst of God's paradise. The overcomer is the one who overcomes all the corrupting influences that threaten the believers in their walk with the Lord. This includes the leaven of wrong doctrine (Galatians 5:9), the leaven of sin (1 Corinthians 5:6-8) and the leaven of hypocrisy (Luke 12:1). John says:

> *"For whatever is born of God overcomes the world. This is the victory that has overcome the world: your faith. [5] Who is he who overcomes the world, but he who believes that Jesus is the Son of God?"* (1 John 5:4-5)

Chapter Two

The reward of overcoming is to eat the tree of life. Jesus planted the tree of life within reach of all who would repent and believe when He died on the cross. He called Himself the true vine (John 15:1) which is a tree with weak branches that must hang on wooden supports. Jesus is the tree of life and we are to feast on Him in this life and enjoy Him forever in the midst of God's paradise. The first one to do so was the thief who died beside Jesus on the cross (Luke 23:43).

Smyrna – the Persecuted Church

"[8] To the angel of the assembly in Smyrna write: "The first and the last, who was dead, and has come to life says these things: [9] "I know your works, oppression, and your poverty (but you are rich), and the blasphemy of those who say they are Jews, and they are not, but are a synagogue of Satan. [10] Don't be afraid of the things which you are about to suffer. Behold, the devil is about to throw some of you into prison, that you may be tested; and you will have oppression for ten days. Be faithful to death, and I will give you the crown of life. [11] He who has an ear, let him hear what the Spirit says to the assemblies. He who overcomes won't be harmed by the second death."

We know from church history that Polycarp was at this time one of the leading elders in this church[9]. He was martyred many years later in 153 AD. He was given the chance to deny Christ and live, but replied "Eighty and six years have I now served Christ, and he has never done me the least wrong: How then can I blaspheme my King and my Saviour?" Polycarp knew John personally and received this wonderful message from Jesus through him. Today Smyrna (modern name Izmir) is the second largest city of Turkey and a large sea port. There is still a living church there to this day.

The word Smyrna derives from the word "myrrh" which was a fragrance oil used as the main ingredient of the anointing oil of the tabernacle

---

[9] E.H. Broadbent, *The Pilgrim Church* (Pickering and Inglis: London, 1931), p. 8.

(Exodus 30:23). It was used in wedding celebrations (Esther 2:12) and also to anoint the dead. Nicodemus laid 100lbs of myrrh and aloes in the tomb of Jesus when he and Joseph of Arimathea buried the Lord (John 19:39). It is entirely appropriate that this is the name of the city linked with a persecuted church. The church in Smyrna was suffering intense persecution and was anointed by God with grace and favour.

The persecution came, at least in part, from those who claimed to be Jews but were of the synagogue of Satan. This is not an anti-Semitic statement since John himself was a Jew. It is a severe denunciation of the evil of all religion without the reality of the presence of God. Jesus had said that the generation in which He lived was evil (Luke 11:29). It is true that the Jews of the first century not only rejected their Messiah but also were the chief persecutors of the church:

> *"For you, brothers, became imitators of the assemblies of God which are in Judea in Christ Jesus; for you also suffered the same things from your own countrymen, even as they did from the Jews;* [15] *who killed both the Lord Jesus and their own prophets, and drove us out, and didn't please God, and are contrary to all men;* [16] *forbidding us to speak to the Gentiles that they may be saved; to fill up their sins always. But wrath has come on them to the uttermost." (1 Thessalonians 2:14-16)*

The same could later be said about the Spanish Inquisition which was conducted in the name of Christianity. Jesus was pointing out the evil of religious people practising wickedness with zeal in the name of God. Just as He asserted that this was a synagogue of Satan and not of God so also it can be true of many religious activities that promote violence, that they have more in common with Satan than with God.

This church at Smyrna needed words of affirmation and encouragement from the Lord. There was no rebuke from the Lord for this church. The believers here were faithfully following their Master and Jesus was speaking to affirm and strengthen them. This church was passing through severe opposition and persecution. They seemed poor in their own sight but were rich in the eyes of God.

The key word of Jesus to this church at Smyrna and to all churches is:

> "Be faithful to death, and I will give you the crown of life."

This word does not only mean that we must be faithful all of our lives, but that we must be willing to lay down our lives for the church, and for the Lord. The Lord Himself loved His church and died for her (Ephesians 5:25). Christians must have this lifestyle that is choosing faithfulness to God above life itself. Bearing the cross, laying down our lives is the distinctive mark of a disciple and everyone who truly loves Jesus Christ.

Jesus foretold greater suffering still to come and urged them not to fear. He foretold they would be in prison for ten days. This may refer to a literal ten days of imprisonment or may indicate that their suffering had a beginning and would also have an end. It is of immense comfort for those passing through trials that God is in control and sets the limits of our pain both in intensity and duration:

> "No temptation has taken you except what is common to man. God is faithful, who will not allow you to be tempted above what you are able, but will with the temptation also make the way of escape, that you may be able to endure it." (1 Corinthians 10:13)

The reward for overcoming would be to escape the second death, which is eternal separation from God in the lake of fire (Revelation 20:14).

Pergamos – False Teaching and Immorality

[12] "To the angel of the assembly in Pergamum write: "He who has the sharp two-edged sword says these things: [13] "I know your works and

where you dwell, where Satan's throne is. You hold firmly to my name, and didn't deny my faith in the days of Antipas my witness, my faithful one, who was killed among you, where Satan dwells. [14] But I have a few things against you, because you have there some who hold the teaching of Balaam, who taught Balak to throw a stumbling block before the children of Israel, to eat things sacrificed to idols, and to commit sexual immorality. [15] So you also have some who hold to the teaching of the Nicolaitans likewise. [16] Repent therefore, or else I am coming to you quickly, and I will make war against them with the sword of my mouth. [17] He who has an ear, let him hear what the Spirit says to the assemblies. To him who overcomes, to him I will give of the hidden manna, and I will give him a white stone, and on the stone a new name written, which no one knows but he who receives it.

The city of Pergamos had a great temple to the god Zeus the chief god in the pantheon of Greek gods and goddesses. This temple was built on the top of a 1000 ft. hill in the centre of the city. Pergamos was also the first city in the Roman Empire to erect a temple to Augustus Caesar. It had renowned medical schools and a temple to the Greek god of health Asclepius which was symbolized by a serpent (still the universal symbol of a pharmacy). It was a rich city with the third largest library in the world (with 300,000 volumes), and many sports facilities and theatres. The archaeologist Sir William Ramsay said of Pergamos that:

> "Beyond all the cities of Asia Minor it gives the traveller the impression of being the home of authority."[10]

The altar of Pergamos, as big as a tennis court, was taken to the Berlin Pergamum museum, where it is to this day. It was taken there at the end of the 19th century and within a few years Germany was at war and destroyed, then at war again, then shattered and divided. While there is probably no link between the location of the altar and the throne of

---

[10] W.M. Ramsay, *The Letters to the Seven Churches of Asia*, p.281. Kissinger Legacy Reprints, 2010

Chapter Two

Satan, yet it is an intriguing fact of history, beyond contradiction, that Germany was a focus for great evil in the first half of the 20th century.

Pergamos was said by Jesus to be the centre of Satan's power with his throne located here. From this, it may be judged that Satan needs physical headquarters to run his kingdom. It is sometimes thought by believers that Satan is omnipresent, or at least is everywhere on planet earth. But the Bible reveals that omnipresence is an attribute of God alone. No created being, whether human or angel shares this quality with God. It is said of Satan in the book of Job:

> *"Yahweh said to Satan, "Where have you come from?" Then Satan answered Yahweh, and said, "From going back and forth in the earth, and from walking up and down in it." (Job 1:7)*

Satan moves from place to place on the earth and though his movements may presumably be extremely swift yet he is confined to one place at any one time.

This church had remained faithful to the Lord through days of persecution. Jesus uses the interesting word "Antipas" to describe one of the early martyrs in this town. The word means literally "against everything." This can sum up the Christian's lot: he is a stranger in every nation and an opposer of every other religion and philosophy. Though he is kind, loving and generous to all, yet in his mind and philosophy he is in direct conflict with the world and the powers of darkness that lie behind the world's systems (1 John 2:15-16). This is the "privilege" of all who would live faithful to Jesus: they will be persecuted (2 Tim 3:12).[11]

---

[11] A second century letter to Diognetus gives the following description of Christians: "They live in the flesh, but they are not governed by the desires of the flesh. They pass their days upon earth, but they are citizens of heaven. Obedient to the laws, they yet live on a level that transcends the law. Christians love all men, but all men persecute them. Condemned because they are not understood, they are put to death, but raised to life again. They live in poverty,

Jesus commended this church but was grieved that despite their many victories there was impurity through the teaching of Balaam. Balaam had prophesied for money paid by the Moabite King Balak (Numbers 22 to 26). Though Balaam knew the God of Israel he used his gifts for financial gain (Numbers 22:7, Jude 1:11). But when Balaam had been unable to curse the people, he advised Balak to send beautiful women among Israel to seduce the men. Balaam had realised that though the people of God could not be overcome by any curse from Satan, yet if they compromised with sin these chosen people would be weak and vulnerable (Numbers 31:16). These are serious warnings in the 21st century when there are many scandals involving misuse of money in the ministry and sexual immorality. Some have even taught that grace will save us no matter what our life-style. This warning is chilling since such liberal values in the church can of themselves draw great numbers. Sinners do not want to renounce worldly carnal pleasures. But the church that would please God must live in purity, through faith and the power of the Holy Spirit.

Jesus offered the church a choice: either to repent and rid themselves of impurity, or Jesus Christ would Himself step in and fight against those who held such corrupting doctrines. The most dangerous position is to make an enemy of Jesus Christ. "If God be for us, who can be against us?" (Romans 8:31). But if God is against us then we are without hope unless and until we repent.

Jesus promised that those who overcome will be given hidden manna – the nourishing of the soul in the secret place of fellowship with God in

---

but enrich many; they are totally destitute, but possess an abundance of everything. They suffer dishonour, but that is their glory. They are defamed, but vindicated. A blessing is their answer to abuse, deference their response to insult. For the good they do they receive the punishment of malefactors, but even then they rejoice, as though receiving the gift of life. They are attacked by the Jews as aliens, they are persecuted by the Greeks, yet no one can explain the reason for this hatred."

prayer. He will also give them a white stone with their name inscribed, a name known only to the one who received it. A white stone was used as a means of entry to many Roman events, and a white stone was also given to a person who was declared innocent in a court of law. These cultural details are fascinating but this verse points to the mystery of personal fellowship with Jesus Christ, leading to knowledge that cannot be shared with others and can only be understood by the person receiving revelation from the Lord.

Thyatira – False teaching and Immorality

[18] "To the angel of the assembly in Thyatira write: "The Son of God, who has his eyes like a flame of fire, and his feet are like burnished brass, says these things: [19] "I know your works, your love, faith, service, patient endurance, and that your last works are more than the first. [20] But I have this against you, that you tolerate your woman, Jezebel, who calls herself a prophetess. She teaches and seduces my servants to commit sexual immorality, and to eat things sacrificed to idols. [21] I gave her time to repent, but she refuses to repent of her sexual immorality. [22] Behold, I will throw her into a bed, and those who commit adultery with her into great oppression, unless they repent of her works. [23] I will kill her children with Death, and all the assemblies will know that I am he who searches the minds and hearts. I will give to each one of you according to your deeds. [24] But to you I say, to the rest who are in Thyatira, as many as don't have this teaching, who don't know what some call 'the deep things of Satan,' to you I say, I am not putting any other burden on you. [25] Nevertheless, hold that which you have firmly until I come. [26] He who overcomes, and he who keeps my works to the end, to him I will give authority over the nations. [27] He will rule them with a rod of iron, shattering them like clay pots; as I also have received of my Father:[28] and I will give him the morning star. [29] He who has an ear, let him hear what the Spirit says to the assemblies."

This was the smallest of the seven cities. It had many trade guilds, which caused many Christian traders to come into a conflict of conscience, since in order to trade they had to participate in heathen religious ceremonies.

Thyatira was in a similar condition to Pergamos, and had works that were greater than in the early days of its founding. It is remarkable that the Lord pointed in each message to the positive things in the assembly before He unveiled what was wrong. The only exception was the church at Laodicea, where Jesus found nothing positive to commend.

Though Thyatira had similar problems to the church in Pergamos, the false teaching was of a greater level and involved a "Jezebel spirit." Some may speculate that this is an attack on the ministry of women, but this cannot be the case. The church is the bride of Christ, but this does not mean that it is only open to females. By the same token there are many men with a "Jezebel spirit" which symbolises a teaching that waters down the message of holiness in the church and permits fornication, adultery and all forms of immorality. While grace is needed in the handling of people who fail, yet there is to be a clear upholding of righteousness and holiness in the churches, not by works of the law, but by grace through faith and empowered by the Holy Spirit. The church must be holy, and attention must be given to the essential foundations of spiritual life rather than secondary issues such as numbers attending a church.

The warning of the Lord to the person or persons ministering in the spirit of Jezebel was that the time for the direct intervention of Jesus had already come. Jesus said that He will cast that minister into a bed of sickness. This must mean that some terrible affliction would come upon them whether mental or physical. The warning was yet more severe for those who were the spiritual offspring of this ministry. They will be killed by death. This is exactly what happened to Ananias and Sapphira in Acts 5:1-11. The Lord will intervene in situations where sin is endangering the existence of the church. God is jealous of His people and those who engage in sin or in teachings that encourage sin are making an enemy of God.

Despite the dire condition of this church, Jesus had a most solemn and remarkable promise. If they overcame they would be given power over the nations to rule them with a rod of iron. God's grace is matchless and humbling as He raises the beggars to be the noblest princes who will rule and reign with Christ Himself.

CHAPTER 3

SARDIS, PHILADELPHIA AND LAODICEA

Sardis – the Church with a Great Name but a Dead Spirit.

Revelation 3:1 *"And to the angel of the assembly in Sardis[12] write: "He who has the seven Spirits of God, and the seven stars says these things: "I know your works, that you have a reputation of being alive, but you are dead. ² Wake up, and keep the things that remain, which you were about to throw away, for I have found no works of yours perfected before my God. ³ Remember therefore how you have received and heard. Keep it, and repent. If therefore you won't watch, I will come as a thief, and you won't know what hour I will come upon you. ⁴ Nevertheless you have a few names in Sardis that did not defile their garments. They will walk with me in white, for they are worthy. ⁵ He who overcomes will be arrayed in white garments, and I will in no way blot his name out of the book of life, and I will confess his name before my Father, and before his angels. ⁶ He who has an ear, let him hear what the Spirit says to the assemblies.*

---

[12] Sardis was a small and unimportant city, which had once been the capital of the ancient kingdom of Lydia. It was famous for dyeing wool garments. The city was destroyed by an earthquake in AD 17, and the Roman government had given 10 million Sesterces to rebuild it and the city of Philadelphia. Philadelphia was nearly renamed "Neocaeserea" in gratitude to the Roman emperor.

Chapter Three

Jesus' message to this church began with the assertion that although they had a great name for themselves, their lives failed to match up to it. Churches generally name themselves according to their core doctrine such as Evangelical, Baptist, Pentecostal or Presbyterian. Sometimes the name will reflect the life style of the church with nouns such as Fellowship or Holiness. Most churches demonstrate a disparity between their name and the reality of the life they lead. Few Pentecostal churches are living in the full power of Acts chapter 2.

Watchman Nee[13] so disliked denominational titles that he refused at last to recognise any of them and acknowledged only the church of a locality, hence the church of Singapore, the church of London etc. Soon of course this "non-denominational name" lost its significance and finally became yet another denomination. Others have thought out the best title believing that it will make a significant contribution: "The True Church of God," "The True Apostolic, Full Gospel, Pentecostal Four Square Assemblies of God." In the end the name means nothing, it is rather the lives of the believers that will make the reputation of the church.

Jesus rebuked this church for having a great name but no life. He declared that their works were not perfected (literally not completed or finished). They never saw things through, they never finished things off. They started but did not finish, and they gave up half way. It may also mean that their works were half-hearted or performed with mixed motives that didn't satisfy God's heart. This church was warned to turn back and remember how God had moved in the past. They were to seek to regain that original freshness by pleading with God for an outpouring of the Holy Spirit. Jesus said that things were ready to die indicating that spiritual decline may reach a stage when spiritual life is completely snuffed out and lost by neglect.

---

[13] Watchman Nee, (1903 – 1972), was a Chinese church leader and Christian teacher during the 20th century and was imprisoned for his faith for the last 20 years of his life.

Jesus warned the church to remember how they had received life in the beginning. There are many exhortations in the scripture to keep alive the memory of past blessings both in our personal lives and in our nation. The Passover and the feast of unleavened bread were instituted to remind subsequent generations of God's amazing miracle in leading the people of Israel out of Egypt (Exodus 13:1-8). In the same way the communion was to be a marker to remind Christians of the sacrifice that lies at the heart of the life of God's people:

> "Take, eat. This is my body, which is broken for you. Do this in memory of me." (1 Corinthians 11:24).

The sad truth is that believers may easily forget their origins or even their conversion. Jesus warned those who were dead spiritually that He would suddenly come upon them like a thief in the night. God can visit an individual or a church at any time, not only at the second coming. Churches may be convulsed when the hidden sins of leaders are revealed, or when divisions or even sickness shake the church. Leviticus 14:34 speaks of a leprous plague on a house and if it has penetrated into the structure it must be demolished and all traces of it removed (Leviticus 14:44-45). A church or a ministry may become leprous and Jesus will come suddenly and deal with it. The severity of God must never be underestimated, but it must also never be thought that God has forgotten to be loving. Love cannot allow churches or ministries to continue uncorrected. God cares for the sheep who are being led astray and also for the ministers themselves and by His actions God seeks to bring back his wandering lambs

Yet even in Sardis there were believers who were faithfully walking in white. Their names were written in the book of life and would not be blotted out.

> "If anyone takes away from the words of the book of this prophecy, may God take away his part from the tree of life, and out of the holy city, which are written in this book." (Rev.22:19)

Chapter Three

The Bible teaches that we are to walk faithfully with the Lord and not lose the great salvation that He has promised us. Some believers have the grief of being in a church where the flame is burning very low, and in such challenging situations each must ensure that they themselves do not lose the fervent love and holiness that accompany living faith.

Philadelphia – literal meaning "brotherly love" – the Church Distinguished by Fervent Love

[7] "To the angel of the assembly in Philadelphia write: "He who is holy, he who is true, he who has the key of David, he who opens and no one can shut, and who shuts and no one opens, says these things:
[8] "I know your works (behold, I have set before you an open door, which no one can shut), that you have a little power, and kept my word, and didn't deny my name. [9] Behold, I give some of the synagogue of Satan, of those who say they are Jews, and they are not, but lie. Behold, I will make them to come and worship before your feet, and to know that I have loved you. [10] Because you kept my command to endure, I also will keep you from the hour of testing, which is to come on the whole world, to test those who dwell on the earth. [11] I am coming quickly! Hold firmly that which you have, so that no one takes your crown. [12] He who overcomes, I will make him a pillar in the temple of my God, and he will go out from there no more. I will write on him the name of my God, and the name of the city of my God, the new Jerusalem, which comes down out of heaven from my God, and my own new name. [13] He who has an ear, let him hear what the Spirit says to the assemblies.

This city still has a Christian witness today. It was to pass through deep trials but it was a worthy church. This is the second of the seven churches with no reproof from the Lord. He reminded them of His sovereign power: He has the key of David and it is He that can prosper a work or cause it to disappear.

Jesus declared that though the church was weak and had little strength, yet it was very precious to Him because they had kept His word. This simply means they were obedient and persistent in their faithful attention to doing what He commanded. Their reward was an open door in the Spirit, in prayer, in preaching, in evangelism, in all realms. One may infer from the name of the city that their obedience to Him was in demonstrating love for each other. The Bible singles out love for God as the first and great commandment, and the second to love our neighbour.

> *"Jesus said to him, "'You shall love the Lord your God with all your heart, with all your soul, and with all your mind.' [38] This is the first and great commandment. [39] A second likewise is this, 'You shall love your neighbor as yourself.' [40] The whole law and the prophets depend on these two commandments."" (Matthew 22:37-40)*

Jesus called it His "new commandment" that believers should love one another with His measure of love:

> "A new commandment I give to you, that you love one another. Just as I have loved you, you also love one another."
> (John 13:34)

Love will always open the door, and love is the great key to growth. Believers are to love sinners, seek out people to help, take opportunities to pour out to people. Such a church will grow and only such a church deserves to grow.

Moreover Jesus promised that He would vindicate this church and show openly to all that they had His approval. Once more the synagogue of Satan was mentioned, describing Jews who had embraced a position of religious bigotry. Though it is not clear how it would happen, Jesus promised He would so vindicate this church that its enemies would be forced to bow down and recognise the love of Jesus Messiah for them.

Jesus then promised these believers that they would be kept from the hour of trial coming on the whole world. Some have related this to the rapture suggesting that the believers would be taken away before the great tribulation. This will be discussed fully at a later point in the book of Revelation. But this cannot be the meaning of this promise since the believers in Philadelphia did not live to see the coming of Christ. It is rather a promise that God alone decides the limits of tribulation and affliction through which we must pass. There will indeed be a period of Great Tribulation before the return of Christ, but it must also be recognised that there have been many periods of great testing for the church in the last two thousand years. For centuries countless believers have died in waves of persecution and have not been spared as these believers were. God will never allow His children to be tested above what they are able to bear.

Laodicea[14] – the Half Hearted Church

[14] "To the angel of the assembly in Laodicea write:
"The Amen, the Faithful and True Witness, the Head of God's creation, says these things:
[15] "I know your works, that you are neither cold nor hot. I wish you were cold or hot. [16] So, because you are lukewarm, and neither hot nor cold, I will vomit you out of my mouth. [17] Because you say, 'I am rich, and have gotten riches, and have need of nothing;' and don't know that you are the wretched one, miserable, poor, blind, and naked; [18] I counsel you to buy from me gold refined by fire, that you may become rich; and white garments, that you may clothe yourself, and that the shame of your nakedness may not be revealed; and eye salve to anoint your eyes, that you may see. [19] As many as I love, I reprove and chasten. Be zealous

---

[14] Laodicea was one of three cities (along with Philadelphia and Sardis) that were destroyed by an earthquake in AD 17. The Roman government had given huge sums of money in aid but Laodicea had rejected the aid, because it was such a wealthy city. Philip the apostle was martyred in the city of Hierapolis not far away.

therefore, and repent. ²⁰ Behold, I stand at the door and knock. If anyone hears my voice and opens the door, then I will come in to him, and will dine with him, and he with me. ²¹ He who overcomes, I will give to him to sit down with me on my throne, as I also overcame, and sat down with my Father on his throne. ²² He who has an ear, let him hear what the Spirit says to the assemblies."

This is the church that has often been taken as the picture of the western church in the 21st century. It was a church that had wealth but no zeal. Jesus said that their lavish wealth had blinded them to their deep need. They were in a piteous state but did not know it. On the contrary they thought they were without need of anything. This diagnosis of the power of riches to dull a soul to spiritual need should provoke all who are wealthy to adjust their life style to align themselves with the Son of God. Jesus said that the "deceitfulness of riches would choke the word of God (Matthew 13:22). Paul said that:

> *"For the love of money is a root of all kinds of evil. Some have been led astray from the faith in their greed, and have pierced themselves through with many sorrows." (1 Timothy 6:10)*

Believers may be dying and yet dangerously unaware of their perilous condition. The word of prophecy was to awaken the church from sleep.

The most terrible condemnation was that there was neither cold indifference nor passionate zeal. Jesus declared that He would vomit the church out of His mouth as repulsive. Christ indicated that if there was coldness in the church He could do something, because souls would realise their need, but lukewarmness produces precisely those drowsy conditions which allow Christians to have enough religion not to fear eternity, but not enough to flee the world. Christ found nothing to praise in this church.

Jesus counselled this church to be zealous. But how may one find zeal if that is precisely what is lacking? The answer is obedience. Jesus was declaring that it lies within our freedom of will to choose to be zealous and we are not merely to passively wait for something to happen. If God commands something then He knows that we are able to obey, otherwise His command would be impossible to fulfil.

There are three aspects to His advice:

1. To buy gold, which symbolises godly character and enduring faith. We are to discard the superficiality of pleasure seeking and answer the high calling to share in the fellowship of Christ's sufferings (Philippians 3:10).

2. To buy white clothing. This is inward purity and heart holiness. We are to transact with God and allow Him to cleanse and purge the inner recesses of our hearts.

3. To buy eye-salve to anoint their eyes. This is revelation from God of the unseen world. Hagar was dying beside a well and it was only when her eyes were opened that she realised the abundant provision right beside her (Genesis 21:19).

The church needed to transact with God on these things. But what is the currency of heaven? How can we buy it? The answer is the currency of the heart: humility, faith, love, repentance and zeal. This is a currency that every person has to hand. But it cannot be used without letting go of things that compete with a life of cross-bearing and uncompromising devotion to Jesus. It must nevertheless be stressed that although we can buy these things by a right attitude of heart, it is through the blood of Christ alone that we are worthy to receive any blessing at all. Our purchasing power is merely the positioning of our soul to receive what Christ died to give us.

Jesus said that He was standing at the door of this church and knocking from the outside. Though this verse may be applied to sinners in evangelism, in its original context it was directed to believers whose lifestyle had led to the exclusion of Jesus from their activities. It is indeed a sobering challenge to ask whether church meetings can run without the blessing of the Lord. Many churches have competent musicians and great communicators who can entertain but this does not guarantee that the Lord is present.

Though Jesus was addressing the church when He said that He was standing outside, yet His invitation was directed to the individuals. The door to a church can only be opened as each member personally relates to the Lord and develops a loving open attitude to Him.

Despite the carnal condition of this church Jesus promised them that if they repent He would grant them the unspeakable honour of ruling with Him and sharing His throne. Oh the depths of the mercy of God! Where sin abounds, grace abounds yet more.

CHAPTER 4

THE CLEAREST VISION OF HEAVEN IN THE BIBLE

Revelation 4:1 *After these things I looked and saw a door opened in heaven, and the first voice that I heard, like a trumpet speaking with me, was one saying, "Come up here, and I will show you the things which must happen after this."*
[2] Immediately I was in the Spirit. Behold, there was a throne set in heaven, and one sitting on the throne [3] that looked like a jasper stone and a sardius. There was a rainbow around the throne, like an emerald to look at. [4] Around the throne were twenty-four thrones. On the thrones were twenty-four elders sitting, dressed in white garments, with crowns of gold on their heads. [5] Out of the throne proceed lightnings, sounds, and thunders. There were seven lamps of fire burning before his throne, which are the seven Spirits of God.

John heard a voice and was carried in the Spirit through an open door into heaven. He was taken there to see the unfolding drama of the cross from heaven's perspective. He was once more in the Spirit, in the consciousness of the unseen world. While few of us will have special experiences like John, being consciously in the Spirit is the privilege of all who will wait quietly in their hearts on the Lord. He was immediately conscious of the throne, the centre of authority in the universe, the place from which all things are directed. Words failed John to describe the One who sat there, and he could only explain the vision of God as being like a precious stone with depths but no precise form or shape. Paul expresses it as follows:

> *"The blessed and only Ruler, the King of kings, and Lord of lords; who alone has immortality, dwelling in unapproachable light; whom no man has seen, nor can see: to whom be honor and eternal power. Amen.." (1 Timothy 6:15-16)*

God dwells in brightness which cannot be penetrated by our gaze and we wonder and worship at the shimmering depths of beauty which are not physical but spiritual. It is the beauty and brightness of God's awesome being. God's throne was surrounded by a perfect circle of a rainbow all around the throne, emerald green, the colour of life. God established the rainbow as a sign of His covenant and sees all things through the perspective of His everlasting covenant.

> *"He always remembers his covenant." (Psalm 111:5)*

In Hebrews 13:20-21 we read:

> *"Now may the God of peace, who brought again from the dead the great shepherd of the sheep with the blood of an eternal covenant, our Lord Jesus, make you complete in every good work to do his will, working in you that which is well pleasing in his sight, through Jesus Christ, to whom be the glory forever and ever. Amen."*

The phrase *"an eternal covenant"* is a further description of the "New Covenant" and introduces us to the fact that though the new covenant is experienced as a means of salvation from sin, yet it has an eternal context that far transcends time. The everlasting covenant is through the blood of Jesus, by which we understand that this covenant is as everlasting as God Himself and is part of His nature and being.

What was the nature of the everlasting covenant before man was introduced to it? There was obviously no written agreement between the three persons of the Godhead. The covenant that binds them together is a bond of perpetual love written in their life blood. The three persons of the Godhead are constantly poured out for one another in living sacrifice, honouring and serving one another in flawless never-ending love. There is no cross in God, no nails, no thorns, but there is the love that will pour itself out to the point of death when need arises. The marvel of the new covenant is that human beings become partakers of the same life and nature that is in God. Humanity is grafted into the Godhead by the blood of the covenant. Humanity does not become divine, but is indwelt by the divine life of God Himself. The act of God in opening the veins of His son was an act of stupendous daring, to open a door for sinners to approach and enter into the very heart of God.

Around the throne were 24 thrones with elders sitting upon them. This may be saints of old such as Abraham and Moses, and it may be that their number is greater than 24 which may simply be symbolic of this group of men and women who have taken their place around the throne. The number 24 occurs in 1 Chronicles 24:7-18 and 25:9-31 where 24 divisions of priests and musicians were appointed to worship in the temple that David planned according to the pattern given him by the Spirit.

> *"Then David gave to Solomon his son the plans for… the temple, and the plans of all that he had by the Spirit, for the courts of Yahweh's house … also for the divisions of the priests and the Levites, for all the work of the service of Yahweh's house" (1 Chronicles 28:11-13)*

From the throne proceeded different kinds of utterance, some like thunder, some like flashes of lightning. Around the throne were the seven lamps representing the seven Spirits of God. The number 7 is suggesting the perfect aspects of the Holy Spirit working in the human race. The Bible indicates there is one Spirit not seven (Ephesians 4:4) and the Bible describes the different aspects of the Holy Spirit with more than seven titles:

> The Spirit of wisdom and understanding, (Isaiah 11:2)
> The Spirit of counsel and might, (Isaiah 11:2)
> The Spirit of knowledge and of the fear of the LORD. (Isaiah 11:2)
> The Spirit of power and of love and of a sound mind. (2 Timothy 1:7, NKJV)
> The Spirit of faith, (2 Corinthians 4:13)
> The Spirit of wisdom and revelation (Ephesians 1:17)
> The Spirit of grace and supplication (Zechariah 12:10)
> The Spirit of glory (1 Peter 4:14)

So once again it is probable that the Bible is indicating through the number seven the complete sufficiency and perfection of the person of the Holy Spirit.

The Sea of Glass

⁶Before the throne was something like a sea of glass, similar to crystal. In the middle of the throne, and around the throne were four living creatures full of eyes before and behind. ⁷The first creature was like a lion, and the second creature like a calf, and the third creature had a face like a man, and the fourth was like a flying eagle. ⁸The four living creatures, each one of them having six wings, are full of eyes around and within. They have no rest day and night, saying, "Holy, holy, holy is the Lord God, the Almighty, who was and who is and who is to come!"

⁹When the living creatures give glory, honor, and thanks to him who sits on the throne, to him who lives forever and ever, ¹⁰the twenty-four elders fall down before him who sits on the throne, and worship him who lives forever and ever, and throw their crowns before the throne, saying, ¹¹"Worthy are you, our Lord and God, the Holy One, to receive the glory, the honor, and the power, for you created all things, and because of your desire they existed, and were created!"

Chapter Four

John seemed to be viewing heaven from a high vantage point. He saw before the throne a lake of such perfect stillness that it was like purest glass as clear as crystal. No impurity clouded its depths and no waves troubled its surface. John would have seen everything reflected in its surface. Then John saw the four living ones that Ezekiel had seen in his vision of heaven (Ezekiel 1:5). This was probably the Seraphim with six wings that Isaiah saw, crying out "Holy, holy, holy" in reaction to the impact of God on their gaze (Isaiah 6:2). These four angels were full of eyes around them and within, symbolising that they were full of sight: foresight, insight, hindsight with nothing capable of escaping their notice. The many eyes symbolise the eternal wisdom and knowledge of Christ whose judgments are true and righteous.

The living ones had each a different face: a lion, a calf, a man and an eagle. The Renaissance painters associated each of the four gospels with one of these creatures.[15] Matthew was associated with the lion (king), Mark with the calf (servant sacrifice), Luke with the man (humanity) and John with the eagle (divinity). It is certainly true that these four gospels displayed the glory of Jesus in four different aspects of His being, and these living ones bear the image of God.

The scene was one of worship poured out to God as the creator (not yet the Redeemer). Their prayer had no mention of the cross and this was the exulted praise of perfect beings recognising the supreme authorship of the universe. This scene was heaven before the cross of Calvary. The sight was about to change, John was not seeing a static tableau but an unfolding drama

.

---

[15] There are many examples to choose from including: Rubens picture of the four evangelists in Schloss Sans Souci, Berlin c. 1614; see also the Book of Kells in Trinity College Dublin which has an illumination of the four evangelists with their symbols c. 800. Different artists attributed the four creatures differently but saw them as representing the fourfold character of Christ through the four gospels.

CHAPTER 5

THE LAMB OPENS THE SCROLL

Revelation 5:1 *"I saw, in the right hand of him who sat on the throne, a book written inside and outside, sealed shut with seven seals. [2] I saw a mighty angel proclaiming with a loud voice, "Who is worthy to open the book, and to break its seals?" [3] No one in heaven above, or on the earth, or under the earth, was able to open the book, or to look in it. [4] And I wept much, because no one was found worthy to open the book, or to look in it. [5] One of the elders said to me, "Don't weep. Behold, the Lion who is of the tribe of Judah, the Root of David, has overcome; he who opens the book and its seven seals." [6] I saw in the middle of the throne and of the four living creatures, and in the middle of the elders, a Lamb standing, as though it had been slain, having seven horns, and seven eyes, which are the seven Spirits of God, sent out into all the earth.*

The drama began with the mention of the scroll in the hand of God. The cry of a strong angel was heard declaring that there was no one worthy to open the story of God's redemptive plan to save mankind. The consequence of this would be that the final phase of the world's history would not be inaugurated. Search was made but no one was found worthy to open it. John wept much realising that this scroll was the story of God's plan to redeem sinners from the power of darkness.

Chapter Five

Imagine for a moment the history of the world if Jesus had not come and died on the cross. There would have been no forgiveness of sins, no cleansing of human hearts, no Holy Spirit revival, no apostles, no church and no gospels with their sublime teaching. Mankind would never have heard the words "love your enemies" and never have heard of the love of God for a fallen world. It is no wonder that John wept and wept, for the world would be a dark place without the revelation of God's heart through His Son Jesus.

Then one of the 24 elders declared the marvelous truth: there was one who had prevailed and was worthy to open the scroll. He heard the words: "the Lion" has prevailed, and looked over the expanse of heaven to the throne and saw not a lion but a lamb as though it had been slain. He looked on the crucified Son of God now enthroned bearing His glorious scars and having seven horns, indicating perfect authority and seven eyes representing the seven-fold perfections of the Holy Spirit sent forth to do the will of the Lamb of God.

[7] Then he came, and he took it out of the right hand of him who sat on the throne. [8] Now when he had taken the book, the four living creatures and the twenty-four elders fell down before the Lamb, each one having a harp, and golden bowls full of incense, which are the prayers of the saints. [9] They sang a new song, saying,

> *"You are worthy to take the book,*
> *and to open its seals:*
> *for you were killed,*
> *and bought us for God with your blood,*
> *out of every tribe, language, people, and nation,*
> *[10] and made us kings and priests to our God,*
> *and we will reign on earth."*

[11] I saw, and I heard something like a voice of many angels around the throne, the living creatures, and the elders; and the number of them was ten thousands of ten thousands, and thousands of thousands; [12] saying

with a loud voice, "Worthy is the Lamb who has been killed to receive the power, wealth, wisdom, strength, honor, glory, and blessing!"
[13] I heard every created thing which is in heaven, on the earth, under the earth, on the sea, and everything in them, saying, "To him who sits on the throne, and to the Lamb be the blessing, the honor, the glory, and the dominion, forever and ever! Amen!"
[14] The four living creatures said, "Amen!" The elders fell down and worshiped.

The Lamb appeared in heaven from Calvary and took the scroll out of God's hand. This was the most intense moment of all eternity as every eye in heaven was fixed upon Jesus Christ having obtained eternal salvation once and for all. The four mighty angels and the 24 elders fell on their faces before the throne, singing a new song. This was not the worship of chapter 4 singing praise to the Creator, this was the song of the redeemed having been cleansed by the blood of the Lamb. Their praise is to the One who has not only removed the cursed stain of sin, but has clothed the redeemed with royal and priestly robes, enabling them to share in God's heavenly life.

By the worship from these exalted beings it is once more demonstrated that Jesus, the Lamb of God, is equal to God Himself. Their worship of the Lamb was unequivocally directed towards Jesus Christ who shared the throne of His Father.

The song of the redeemed provoked a loud thunder of praise from countless millions of angels and from the vast number of the redeemed throughout the realms of earth and sea and sky. The songs were a joyous focusing of all creation on the person of Jesus, offering everything they possess to Him because of the immeasurable merit that is His because of His redeeming sacrifice. Heaven itself was filled with anticipation of all that must follow from this amazing act of God.

Chapter Five

Throughout two thousand years of church history, songs have echoed the same paean of praise to the Lamb blending their voices with the throngs of heaven:

> *Were the whole realm of nature mine,*
> *That were an offering far too small,*
> *Love so amazing, so divine,*
> *Demands my soul, my life, my all.*

CHAPTER 6

THE COUNTDOWN BEGINS: THE TIMELINE OF REVELATION

As described earlier, Revelation chapter 6 to 11 provides the reader with the sequence of events from the cross to the return of Christ. Before looking at the specific meaning of the seals and the trumpets it is helpful to grasp the underlying significance of the images of seals and trumpets.

The first great lesson is that all major turning points in world history are triggered by decisions made by God Himself on the throne of the universe. God alone decides the course of human history. Satan is not in sovereign control of any part of history.

The second lesson is that history is not a gentle evolutionary rise from one generation to another. History is punctuated by seismic shifts that shake the human race. This is true on a large scale and also on a personal level. Human beings appear suddenly on the stage of history at birth and depart just as abruptly by their death. In the process of human life sudden great trials and afflictions fall upon individuals with little or no warning. These include sickness, bereavement, financial catastrophes and deep moral lapses. It also includes sudden positive turning points, including conversion, baptism with the Holy Spirit, marriage, the arrival of children, visions, anointings and other miraculous interventions.

The seals and trumpets of Revelation relate to sudden events on the level of world history. A brief glance at the past quickly informs us that we are unable to predict the future because of completely unforeseeable sudden events that change the world for ever. Revivals have changed nations as the great revival of the first century transformed the Roman Empire. Equally the Reformation changed Europe in an incredibly brief span of time. The Wall Street Crash of 29 October 1929 reverberated around the globe spreading bankruptcies and unemployment across the whole world. The French Revolution of 1789, the October Russian Revolution of 1917, the 1st and 2nd world wars changed the lives of millions and had consequences that still resound till today. It is said that when Chairman Mao Tse Tung was asked what he thought about the French Revolution he answered "It's too early to say!"

The first use of the atomic bomb on 6 August (Hiroshima) and the plutonium bomb on 9 August (Nagasaki) 1945 changed the world for ever. What is also striking about these events is the extraordinary timing. If nuclear physics had progressed just a few years earlier then Hitler and Stalin may also have had nuclear weapons at their disposal for use in the Second World War. God opened that seal at a moment when it would warn the world and steer it away from its self-destructive madness. There is sadly no guarantee that this will be the only use of such weapons in the course of future human history.

The attack on the twin towers of September 11th 2001 has echoed around the world triggering wars and conflicts in several nations. The list of such catastrophic events is endless and one is forced to conclude that there could have been dozens of seals and trumpets if all the details of human history were included in the prophecy of Revelation.

In fact, these seals and trumpets are to be taken as giving the key to the understanding of the flow of human history. God allows these events and they can all be understood in the context of these seven.

The First Seal – The White Horse: Outpourings of the Holy Spirit.[16]

***Revelation 6:1** I saw that the Lamb opened one of the seven seals, and I heard one of the four living creatures saying, as with a voice of thunder, "Come and see!" [2] And behold, a white horse, and he who sat on it had a bow. A crown was given to him, and he came out conquering, and to conquer.*

The first event following the cross and the resurrection was the outpouring of the Holy Spirit at Pentecost. White is the colour of Christ and the righteousness of God and of the saints. The crown on the head of this conqueror is a Greek word "stephanos" which is the victor's laurel wreath granted to those who have won a race in the Olympics. The Antichrist wears crowns (Rev 13:1) but this is the Greek word "diadem" and is the crown worn by earth's rulers. Some have speculated that the white horse might be a false prophet but there is no such movement following the events of Calvary. False religions have arisen suddenly in world history and shaken the planet with religious wars and deceptions but there is no strong internal evidence in this verse to force one to interpret it in that manner.

There are several compelling reasons to interpret this as the gospel going forth in revival power:

---

[16] I have been simple and straightforward in my interpretation of the white horse. It is incontrovertible that the first act of God after the death, resurrection and ascension of Christ was the sending forth of the Holy Spirit to apply that victory to whoever would believe. Nevertheless like all interpreters I must acknowledge that I may be wrong and so humbly ask my readers to bear with my interpretation. There are many distinguished authors who take a very different view. I refrain from offering multiple interpretations simply because it would make this commentary unnecessarily long. There are other books that ably fulfil that task. See my brief bibliography at the end of this book.

- It is indisputable that the first event after the death, resurrection and ascension of Jesus was the outpouring of the Holy Spirit on the day of Pentecost. It could be that this is implied in the wave of praise that follows the cross described in chapter 5. But it is possible that this event is described by the first horse.
- God is always the Alpha and Omega. The first seal is Christ and the last seal is the judgments of God on the earth culminating in the coming of Christ.
- Furthermore the single most powerful event in world history was the day of Pentecost, when all the power of the death and resurrection of Jesus were poured out into human hearts creating a new humanity and changing history forever. It would be unusual if this history changing event were not prominent in the book of Revelation.

The Second Seal - War

³When he opened the second seal, I heard the second living creature saying, "Come!" ⁴Another came out, a red horse. To him who sat on it was given power to take peace from the earth, and that they should kill one another. There was given to him a great sword.

War shakes the planet at regular intervals. *"Cry 'Havoc!', and let slip the dogs of war."*[17] This was the cry of Mark Anthony in Shakespeare's Julius Caesar but in reality it does not lie within man's power to start wars. It is vastly comforting to know that wars are limited by the sovereign will and plan of God. Red is indeed the colour of the devil (Revelation 12:3) and it is from Satan that wars spread across the planet but only when God allows it. Later on at the sixth trumpet demons are released to gather the nations together for the final war of Armageddon. If God had

---

[17] Mark Anthony in Act 3, Scene 1, line 273 of William Shakespeare's *Julius Caesar*

not restrained the power of Satan the whole world would be a constant cockpit of fierce and cruel violence on a scale vaster than we have ever seen: *"He makes wars cease to the end of the earth" Psalm46:9 NKJV* .

The Third Seal – Famine

⁵ When he opened the third seal, I heard the third living creature saying, "Come and see!" And behold, a black horse, and he who sat on it had a balance in his hand. ⁶ I heard a voice in the middle of the four living creatures saying, "A measure of wheat for a denarius, and three measures of barley for a denarius! Don't damage the oil and the wine!"

The black horse is the release of starvation on the earth through scarcity. Though the price of wheat and barley shall rocket in this famine, the price of luxury goods such as oil and wine shall be untouched. An example of this would be during the awful famines in Russia in 1921-22 and 1932-33, when the Communist party bosses were still enjoying luxury goods imported from the west.

The Fourth Seal – Death through famines, wars, plagues and wild animals.

⁷ When he opened the fourth seal, I heard the fourth living creature saying, "Come and see!" ⁸ And behold, a pale horse, and he who sat on it, his name was Death. Hades followed with him. Authority over one fourth of the earth, to kill with the sword, with famine, with death, and by the wild animals of the earth was given to him.

The world is frequently rocked with outbreaks of deadly plagues:

- The Black Death of 1348 to 1350 is estimated to have killed 30–60% of Europe's population. The plague may have reduced the world population from an estimated 450 million down to 350–375 million.

- The Spanish flu pandemic of 1918, the deadliest flu epidemic in history, infected an estimated 500 million people worldwide—about one-third of the planet's population—and killed an estimated 20 to 50 million victims.
- Since the beginning of the AIDS epidemic, more than 70 million people have been infected with the HIV virus and about 35 million people have died. Globally, approximately 36.9 million people were living with HIV at the end of 2017.

The description of this fourth seal does not limit its scope to disease but includes war, famine and wild animals.

The Fifth Seal - Persecution

⁹ When he opened the fifth seal, I saw underneath the altar the souls of those who had been killed for the Word of God, and for the testimony of the Lamb which they had. ¹⁰ They cried with a loud voice, saying, "How long, Master, the holy and true, until you judge and avenge our blood on those who dwell on the earth?" ¹¹ A long white robe was given to each of them. They were told that they should rest yet for a while, until their fellow servants and their brothers, who would also be killed even as they were, should complete their course.

Persecution of the Christian church has taken place throughout the last two thousand years with little respite. Waves of tribulation come and go with varying degrees of intensity. Wherever the gospel has penetrated nations there has nearly always been a violent backlash. This began with the church in Judea. Acts tells of the first martyrs at the hands of the Jewish authorities. As the first century progressed it was the Roman state that became the main opponent of Christianity, with thousands including the apostles Peter and Paul dying at the hands of Nero.[18] There were frequent persecutions at the hands of the Roman emperors but in 385 AD a series of executions took place in Trieste at

---

[18] K.S. Latourette, *A History of Christianity vol 1*, p.85. Harper Press 1953.

the hands of church Bishops. The victims were in the Spirit of the reformers of the 16th century,[19] and so began a long history of persecution of Bible believing Christians at the hands of the institutional church. Later centuries have seen the persecution, imprisonment and torture of Christians at the hands of communist governments all over the world.

The Sixth Seal – Cosmic Disturbances

[12] *I saw when he opened the sixth seal, and there was a great earthquake. The sun became black as sackcloth made of hair, and the whole moon became as blood.* [13] *The stars of the sky fell to the earth, like a fig tree dropping its unripe figs when it is shaken by a great wind.* [14] *The sky was removed like a scroll when it is rolled up. Every mountain and island were moved out of their places.* [15] *The kings of the earth, the princes, the commanding officers, the rich, the strong, and every slave and free person, hid themselves in the caves and in the rocks of the mountains.* [16] *They told the mountains and the rocks, "Fall on us, and hide us from the face of him who sits on the throne, and from the wrath of the Lamb,* [17] *for the great day of his wrath has come; and who is able to stand?"*

[17] *"For the great day of His wrath has come, and who is able to stand?"*

The sixth seal is the hardest to interpret. It is a series of cosmic events of extraordinary magnitude, including a very powerful earthquake, and changes to the sun, moon and stars. The reference to stars falling may signify asteroids or comets striking the earth. It might be that these cosmic disturbances are perceived by humanity and are indicating changes in the earth's atmosphere rather than in the stars. The point is that the heavenly bodies are shaken in such a dramatic way that the whole earth knows that judgment is on its way.

---

[19] The most famous of these martyrs was Priscillian from Spain, a deeply devout man with a love for the scriptures. E.H. Broadbent, *The Pilgrim Church,* Pickering & Inglis, 1931 p.37.

Chapter Six

The seventh seal (described in chapter 8) is the outpouring of judgments on the earth immediately preceding the return of Christ. The result of these cosmic disturbances following the sixth seal is to instill the fear of God and impending judgment on all classes of society.

In concluding our thoughts on these first six seals it is remarkable how they fit in with the Olivet discourse. Jesus foretold that the gospel must first be preached to all nations (Matthew 24:14). He described wars, famines and earthquakes in various places (Matthew 24:6-8). He described coming tribulation and persecution (Matthew 24:9) and finally described the shaking of the powers of the heavens (Matthew 24:29).

CHAPTER 7

THE MULTITUDES OF THE REDEEMED

The Calm Before the Storm

Revelation 7:1 *After this, I saw four angels standing at the four corners of the earth, holding the four winds of the earth, so that no wind would blow on the earth, or on the sea, or on any tree.* [2] *I saw another angel ascend from the sunrise, having the seal of the living God. He cried with a loud voice to the four angels to whom it was given to harm the earth and the sea,* [3] *saying, "Don't harm the earth, neither the sea, nor the trees, until we have sealed the bondservants of our God on their foreheads!"*

Chapter 7 describes the calm before the storm of God's wrath is poured out on the nations. This chapter is a parallel of Ezekiel 9 when the prophet saw a man with an inkhorn sent out to put a mark on the forehead of the faithful believers of Israel. All who were marked were spared from the angel of judgment passing through the land. Judgment is held back till the time is ripe and God's people have been readied to come through the storms of divine judgment unscathed.

The people of God were sealed in their foreheads. This is the opposite of the sign of the beast who also marks those who worship him in their foreheads (see Revelation 13:16; 20:4). This seal of God's people is not a physical mark, nor a chip implant. The Greek word describes the seal used to imprint the crest and identity of an individual or a government. It was pressed into hot wax and like a coin would leave the outline of the head, or the letters and symbols identifying the owner. All believers are sealed with the Holy Spirit:

> *"Now he who establishes us with you in Christ, and anointed us, is God; who also sealed us, and gave us the down payment of the Spirit in our hearts." (2 Corinthians 1:21-22)*
> *"Christ in whom, having also believed, you were sealed with the promised Holy Spirit" (Ephesians 1:13)*
> *"Don't grieve the Holy Spirit of God, in whom you were sealed for the day of redemption." (Ephesians 4:30)*

The seal of God is on all His people to keep us from the coming judgment.

144,000 from the Tribes of Israel.

[4] I heard the number of those who were sealed, one hundred forty-four thousand, sealed out of every tribe of the children of Israel:
[5] of the tribe of Judah were sealed twelve thousand,
of the tribe of Reuben twelve thousand,
of the tribe of Gad twelve thousand,
[6] of the tribe of Asher twelve thousand,
of the tribe of Naphtali twelve thousand,
of the tribe of Manasseh twelve thousand,
[7] of the tribe of Simeon twelve thousand,
of the tribe of Levi twelve thousand,
of the tribe of Issachar twelve thousand,
[8] of the tribe of Zebulun twelve thousand,
of the tribe of Joseph twelve thousand,
of the tribe of Benjamin were sealed twelve thousand.

The twelve tribes of Israel indicate those whom God has called from the ethnic seed of Abraham. It is an often repeated truth in the Bible, that not all who are of the blood line of Abraham are spiritually sons of Abraham.

> *"For they are not all Israel, that are of Israel. [7] Neither, because they are Abraham's offspring, are they all children."*
> *(Romans 9:6-7)*

Moreover it is also clearly asserted that all who are of faith are of Abraham whether Jew or Gentile.

> *"For this cause it is of faith, that it may be according to grace, to the end that the promise may be sure to all the offspring, not to that only which is of the law, but to that also which is of the faith of Abraham, who is the father of us all." (Romans 4:16)*

The distinction between those of ethnic Israel and the nations is to indicate a difference of background, and does not indicate a distinction that continues into the church and into eternity. All the Gentiles who are of faith are included and absorbed into the Israel of God, which is made up of Jews and Gentiles in one body. In this new body of Christ:

> *"There is neither Jew nor Greek, there is neither slave nor free man, there is neither male nor female; for you are all one in Christ Jesus. [29] If you are Christ's, then you are Abraham's offspring and heirs according to promise." (Galatians 3:28-29)*

God was unambiguous in making it clear that the church and Israel are one and the same by allowing the beginning of the church to be exclusively Jewish. No Gentiles were added to the church until Cornelius was converted in Acts 10. This was followed by the conversion of many Greeks in Acts 11:19-21. This was a huge shock to the early believers who had assumed that the church was, and would remain, completely Jewish. In fact the church was about to face huge challenges as it learned to be one people of God in Christ. This is still a challenge to this day not only between Jews and Gentiles, but between other ethnic groups too.

Paul preached to the Jew first, so it is no surprise that God records here His faithfulness to that part of the human race. The number is 144,000 which is symbolic of perfection and completion and there is no reason to suppose that this number is literal. Paul speaks in Romans of God's plan to save a remnant of the Jews and refers to this remnant as "all Israel":

> *"And so all Israel will be saved. Even as it is written,*
> *"There will come out of Zion the Deliverer,*
>   *and he will turn away ungodliness from Jacob.*
> *This is my covenant to them,*
>   *when I will take away their sins." (Romans 11:26-27)*

These verses speaks of a future act of God in turning many Jews back to living faith in Christ their Messiah. This is what was also revealed to John in Revelation 7, that there will be large number of Jews saved preceding the return of Jesus and preceding the last judgments that are poured out. Paul writes of his hope that if many Jews turn to Jesus it will be a major sign to the human race that Jesus is the Messiah.

> *"Now if their fall is the riches of the world, and their loss the riches of the Gentiles; how much more their fullness?"*
> *(Romans 11:12)*

It will trigger a larger turning to Christ in all nations. There is hope from this chapter of a revival in Israel and a world-wide revival immediately preceding the return of Christ. The future holds many wonderful acts of God that He has already carefully planned.

Revelation 7 has produced a unique list excluding Ephraim and Dan, but including Manasseh, Joseph and Levi.[20] The exclusion of Dan may be because his name means "judge" and in heaven judgment has passed. Manasseh is included and means "forgetting" and in heaven all the woes and pains of earth are forgotten forever. Ephraim means "fruitful" but is replaced with Joseph. The name Ephraim was used in the Old Testament as a synonym for the northern kingdom. For this reason Ephraim was representative of the worst corruption of the 10 tribes.

"Ephraim will become a desolation in the day of rebuke. Among the tribes of Israel, I have made known that which will surely be" (Hosea 5:9)

Joseph on the other hand has the beauty and fragrance of a beautiful life full of forgiveness and grace.

The choice of the twelve tribes confirms the symbolic nature of this list. It would be extraordinary if none from the tribes of Dan and Ephraim were saved on the final day. So the list symbolises all the elect from Israel redeemed and glorified in heaven.

The Innumerable Multitude from all Nations

[9] After these things I looked, and behold, a great multitude, which no man could number, out of every nation and of all tribes, peoples, and languages, standing before the throne and before the Lamb, dressed in white robes, with palm branches in their hands. [10] They cried with a loud voice, saying, "Salvation be to our God, who sits on the throne, and to the Lamb!"
[11] All the angels were standing around the throne, the elders, and the four living creatures; and they fell on their faces before his throne, and worshiped God, [12] saying, "Amen! Blessing, glory, wisdom, thanksgiving, honor, power, and might, be to our God forever and ever! Amen."

---

[20] See Appendix 2 for a comparison of different lists of the tribes at different points in the Bible.

Chapter Seven

John looked again and saw an innumerable multitude suggesting that there will be billions of saved people from all the nations. In the 21st century Christians are derided and marginalized and in many nations bitterly persecuted. Yet the influence and breadth of Christianity is far greater than can be seen in the history books of men. Politicians build their sandcastles to impress their generation, but all these empires will be swept away and only when the veil is lifted will it be revealed what a marvelous and eternal work God has been doing in the hearts and lives of individuals, building a kingdom that shall never pass away.

The multitudes acknowledge God as the owner and sole source of salvation. They worship God in the deep awareness that their salvation is by grace alone. The praises of this huge host cause the angels, the 24 elders and the seraphim to fall down in worship at the greatness of God revealed in this vast host. The salvation of sinners brings glory to God, and the great size of this heavenly throng is fitting to the greatness and majesty of the author and finisher of salvation. God is wonderful and the depth and power of His magnificence are waiting to be revealed when believers are gathered together in heaven to praise and worship God.

Purified in the Fires of Great Tribulation.

[13] One of the elders answered, saying to me, "These who are arrayed in white robes, who are they, and from where did they come?"
[14] I told him, "My lord, you know."
He said to me, "These are those who came out of the great tribulation. They washed their robes, and made them white in the Lamb's blood. [15] Therefore they are before the throne of God, they serve him day and night in his temple. He who sits on the throne will spread his tabernacle over them. [16] They will never be hungry, neither thirsty any more; neither will the sun beat on them, nor any heat; [17] for the Lamb who is in the middle of the throne shepherds them, and leads them to springs of waters of life. And God will wipe away every tear from their eyes."

Jesus said that His return to earth and the rapture of the saints will follow the great tribulation:

> *"But immediately after the oppression (tribulation) of those days, the sun will be darkened, the moon will not give its light, the stars will fall from the sky, and the powers of the heavens will be shaken; ³⁰ and then the sign of the Son of Man will appear in the sky. Then all the tribes of the earth will mourn, and they will see the Son of Man coming on the clouds of the sky with power and great glory. ³¹ He will send out his angels with a great sound of a trumpet, and they will gather together his chosen ones from the four winds, from one end of the sky to the other." (Matthew 24:29-31)*

The phrase "the great tribulation" refers to the universality of this final period of persecution. It will be the epoch of wide spread torture and execution of multitudes of believers. This level of persecution has been steadily rising over the course of the last hundred years and yet is hardly ever reported in the western media.[21] The number of martyrs in Communist countries and the Middle East has never been properly documented. Over the past 2000 years Christians have been thrown to wild animals, burnt alive, imprisoned in labour camps, crucified and cruelly tortured. It is of no comfort to any dying tortured believer to assure them that the last generation will not suffer but will be raptured. The comfort of the word of God lies in the assurance that God sets the limits of persecution and also gives the strength to bear it. Paul suffered fierce opposition and was stoned almost to death in Lystra. He rose up with supernatural refreshing and returned to Lystra to teach the new believers:

---

[21] Many books have described the silent holocaust of Christians e.g. *The Persecution and Genocide of Christians in the Middle East: Prevention, Prohibition, and Prosecution*. Ronald J. Rychlak and Jane F. Adolphe, editors. Anglico Press, 2017.

Chapter Seven

> *"Strengthening the souls of the disciples, exhorting them to continue in the faith, and saying, "We must through many tribulations enter the kingdom of God.""* (Acts 14:22 NKJV)

Believers throughout the centuries have drawn strength from the promise of God to use even negative things for His glory and their blessing.

> *"We know that all things work together for good for those who love God, to those who are called according to his purpose.."* (Romans 8:28)

Paul recorded this promise for believers to give them perspective on the negative things that would befall them. Though there will be a final period of great tribulation, there have been many periods over the centuries and this great multitude includes people from every era who have suffered for the name of Jesus.

John records here 5 promises for believers who persevere through sufferings:
1. They shall experience the full power of the blood to cleanse their hearts. Suffering brings wrong reactions to the surface and this must not discourage us but motivate us to seek the deeper work of the Spirit to transform our lives.
2. They shall be rewarded with direct access to God's throne.
3. They shall know God's presence and indwelling in its full power.
4. Suffering will give way to perfect peace and joy in heaven with God's abundant provision.
5. The Lamb will personally attend to their welfare and wipe away the tears of pain and suffering.

These are promises that are given to all believers but they are of deepest relevance and comfort to those suffering for the name of Jesus.

CHAPTER 8

THE SEVENTH SEAL: GOD'S JUDGMENTS

When a seal is opened it releases things on the earth that continue through the history of the world until the return of Christ.

Taking the 20th century as an example:

1st Seal: The Welsh Revival in 1904 and the Azusa Street Revival in 1906 spreading to nearly every nation.
2nd Seal: 1st and 2nd world wars 1914-1945
3rd Seal: Famines in Russia, China, Ethiopia and in many countries.
4th Seal: Spanish Flu 1919; Aids epidemic 1980s till today.
5th Seal: the persecutions in Communist, Muslim and Hindu countries.

It is possible to see these five seals repeatedly in the history of the world. But the 6th seal has not been fulfilled. There have been no major cosmic disturbances in space. The sun, moon and stars continue unscathed and there is little evidence of the opening of this seal. Equally there is only partial evidence of the natural disasters that are described with the opening of the 7th and the sounding of the seven trumpets. Natural disasters have been part of earth's history for thousands of years. But these trumpets indicate a rapid and progressive countdown of global catastrophes preceding the return of Christ.

Chapter Eight

The Prayers of the Saints

***Revelation 8:1** When he opened the seventh seal, there was silence in heaven for about half an hour. ² I saw the seven angels who stand before God, and seven trumpets were given to them. ³ Another angel came and stood over the altar, having a golden censer. Much incense was given to him, that he should add it to the prayers of all the saints on the golden altar which was before the throne. ⁴ The smoke of the incense, with the prayers of the saints, went up before God out of the angel's hand. ⁵ The angel took the censer, and he filled it with the fire of the altar, and threw it on the earth. There followed thunders, sounds, lightnings, and an earthquake.*
⁶ The seven angels who had the seven trumpets prepared themselves to sound.

The first thing that John saw after the opening of the seventh seal was the awesome silence that filled heaven. God does not send destruction and judgment lightly. He waits till there is no other option. Then John saw the prayers of believers offered with incense on a golden altar before God's throne. These are fragrant beautiful prayers that reach God's heart. They are prayers for the repentance of the nations and for the grace and mercy of God. They are answered by the outpouring of the Holy Spirit in revival, but they are also answered by God's activity in allowing natural disasters to warn the human race of the coming great and terrible day of the Lord. The human race is hurtling in a downwards spiral into moral chaos and rebellion. By acts of judgment God seeks to awaken the human race from its spiritual slumber. God is love and cannot cease to be love. God's judgments are also motivated by His love for lost sinners.

Natural Disasters Shake Planet Earth

The timeline of Revelation runs from chapter 6 to chapter 11. Chapters 12-19 fill in details and describe the main players on the stage of world history. The second coming of Christ is described at the end of chapter

11 and again in chapter 19. Similarly the judgments that strike the earth leading up to the return of Christ are described in chapter 8 and again in chapter 16. Here is a comparison of the two lists:

	Strikes (Ch. 8-11)		Strikes (Ch. 16)
Trumpet 1	earth	Vial 1	earth
Trumpet 2	sea	Vial 2	sea
Trumpet 3	rivers	Vial 3	rivers
Trumpet 4	sun	Vial 4	sun
Trumpet 5	release of demons	Vial 5	torment
Trumpet 6	Euphrates	Vial 6	Euphrates
Trumpet 7	Return of Christ	Vial 7	The end

Though there are differences between chapters 8 and 16 there are significant similarities as a quick comparison shows. Why do we believe they describe the same events from a different perspective?

- The first four trumpets/vials are disasters affecting the earth, the sea, the rivers and the sun. There are some differences but these can be understood as seeing the same event from a different perspective. (For a full harmonisation of the trumpets and the vials see chapter 16).

- The fifth trumpet describes the opening of the bottomless pit and a cloud of demons being released. The fifth vial complements this description showing the torment of the demons as they afflict the kingdom of Antichrist. This event is difficult to imagine since it is described from the spiritual unseen world. Demons will have been bound since the pre-flood days when they overstepped their permitted realm of operation (Jude verse 6). Their effect is torment. What this event would look like in history is difficult to imagine. In the sixties there was a flood of drugs and sexual liberation that destroyed a generation. Was this a flood of demons?

- The sixth trumpet describes a major event centred on the river Euphrates opening the way for the kings of the East to march with an enormous army of 200 million. The sixth vial also describes an event centred on the river Euphrates that opens the door for Armageddon.

- The seventh trumpet describes the coming of Christ and the beginning of the millennium (the kingdoms of this world have become the kingdoms of Christ and He shall reign for ever and ever.) The seventh vial declares that "it is done (or finished)."

The First Trumpet

[7] The first sounded, and there followed hail and fire, mixed with blood, and they were thrown to the earth. One third of the earth was burnt up, and one third of the trees were burnt up, and all green grass was burnt up.

The first area of natural disaster strikes the earth. One third of trees are burnt probably through forest fires caused by a severe world-wide drought that causes all the grass to turn brown.

The Second Trumpet

[8] The second angel sounded, and something like a great burning mountain was thrown into the sea. One third of the sea became blood, [9] and one third of the living creatures which were in the sea died. One third of the ships were destroyed.

The second disaster could be caused by a comet or asteroid striking the ocean and causing a world-wide poisoning of the oceans, and also causing the violent destruction of ships perhaps through tidal waves and tumultuous weather. The colour of the sea is also altered by this cataclysmic event.

The Third Trumpet

[10] The third angel sounded, and a great star fell from the sky, burning like a torch, and it fell on one third of the rivers, and on the springs of the waters. [11] The name of the star is called "Wormwood." One third of the waters became wormwood. Many people died from the waters, because they were made bitter.

The third disaster strikes the water cycle of the planet affecting drinking water. The word Chernobyl in Russian and Ukrainian is the name of the plant "Aretimisa vulgaris" which is a species of wormwood. The Chernobyl disaster sent vast quantities of radioactive particles into the atmosphere which then fell as rain over many parts of Europe as far away as the Lake District in the UK. It would be wrong to assume that Chernobyl was the fulfillment of this prophecy but it would be blind not to connect the proliferation of nuclear weapons and power stations with the possibility of further massive levels of pollution in the future. The Fukushima catastrophe demonstrates how unexpectedly the forces of nature can wreck the most sophisticated of safety defences. Nuclear waste persists for thousands of years and scientists are unable to protect the human race from the inconvenient violence of nature that is beyond their control.

The Fourth Trumpet

[12] The fourth angel sounded, and one third of the sun was struck, and one third of the moon, and one third of the stars; so that one third of them would be darkened, and the day wouldn't shine for one third of it, and the night in the same way.

The fourth calamity affects the atmosphere darkening the world. Chapter 8 does not describe the adverse effects of this change in the climate of the planet, merely documenting the world-wide consequences.

The Fifth, Sixth and Seventh Trumpets

[13] I saw, and I heard an eagle, flying in mid heaven, saying with a loud voice, "Woe! Woe! Woe for those who dwell on the earth, because of the other voices of the trumpets of the three angels, who are yet to sound!"

Chapter 8 ends with the cry of the angel declaring that the last three trumpets are to be the most severe of all.

CHAPTER 9

THE FIFTH TRUMPET: A FLOOD OF DEMONS

Release of Demons and the Final battle of Armageddon.

The Fifth Trumpet: the Bottomless Pit is Opened

Revelation 9:1 *The fifth angel sounded, and I saw a star from the sky which had fallen to the earth. The key to the pit of the abyss was given to him. [2] He opened the pit of the abyss, and smoke went up out of the pit, like the smoke from a burning furnace. The sun and the air were darkened because of the smoke from the pit. [3] Then out of the smoke came locusts on the earth, and power was given to them, as the scorpions of the earth have power. [4] They were told that they should not hurt the grass of the earth, neither any green thing, neither any tree, but only those people who don't have God's seal on their foreheads. [5] They were given power, not to kill them, but to torment them for five months. Their torment was like the torment of a scorpion, when it strikes a person. [6] In those days people will seek death, and will in no way find it. They will desire to die, and death will flee from them. [7] The shapes of the locusts were like horses prepared for war. On their heads were something like golden crowns, and their faces were like people's faces. [8] They had hair like women's hair, and their teeth were like those of lions. [9] They had breastplates, like breastplates of iron. The sound of* *their wings was like the sound of chariots, or of many horses rushing to war. ¹⁰ They have tails like those of scorpions, and stings. In their tails they have power to harm men for five months. ¹¹ They have over them as king the angel of the abyss. His name in Hebrew is "Abaddon", but in Greek, he has the name "Apollyon".*

The bottomless pit is mentioned in several places in the New Testament. In Luke 8:31 the demons begged Jesus not to send them into the abyss which is the anglicised form of the Greek word "abussos" meaning bottomless deep:

> *"They begged him that he would not command them to go into the abyss." (Luke 8:31)*

The parallel scripture in Matthew adds that the demons saw the bottomless pit as a place where they would be tormented:

> *"Behold, they cried out, saying, "What do we have to do with you, Jesus, Son of God? Have you come here to torment us before the time?" (Matthew 8:29)*

Verse 11 describes Satan as the king of the bottomless pit, but this does not mean that it is a kingdom that he rules since in Revelation 20 he is imprisoned there against his will. Jude informs us of angels imprisoned in darkness:

> *"Angels who didn't keep their first domain, but deserted their own dwelling place, he has kept in everlasting bonds under darkness for the judgment of the great day. " (Jude 1:6)*

It is not specified by Jude who these angels are or when they were imprisoned. It is possible that these angels are the "sons of God" mentioned in Genesis 6:2-4 and that these demonic beings have been bound since the days of the flood.

Satan will suffer this punishment during the millennium:

> *"I saw an angel coming down out of heaven, having the key of the abyss and a great chain in his hand. ² He seized the dragon, the old serpent, which is the devil and Satan, who deceives the whole inhabited earth, and bound him for a thousand years, ³ and cast him into the abyss, and shut it, and sealed it over him, that he should deceive the nations no more, until the thousand years were finished. After this, he must be freed for a short time." (Revelation 20:1-3)*

From these scriptures we understand that fallen angels have been imprisoned in the past for their transgressions and that they will be released again to fulfill a role that God has ordained in His sovereign plan.

The demons are described in graphic terms by John as having a fierce and terrifying appearance. Some of the details are incomprehensible to our natural minds. Few people have ever seen angels or demons, but there are some possible exceptions, though these are for obvious reasons unverifiable. (Martin Luther is said to have seen the devil during his stay at the Wartburg and to have thrown an inkwell at the apparition). Here are some of the key elements that are revealed here about these fallen beings:

1. They are granted power, but do not have any unless it is granted them, (verse 4).
2. God commands them and they must obey though they oppose Him, (verse 4).
3. They have no power over life or death. That belongs to God alone, (verse 5).
4. Their form, though invisible to the human eye, is a terrifying mixture of things that harm including the tearing teeth of a lion (verse 8) and the tormenting sting of the scorpion (verse 10)
5. Their king is Satan whose name is Abaddon meaning in Hebrew "destruction" and Apollyon meaning "one who destroys."

Chapter Nine

> Abaddon appears in the Old Testament as another title of hell. *("Hell (Hebrew "Sheol") and Destruction (Hebrew "Abaddon") are before the LORD; So how much more the hearts of the sons of men." (Proverbs 15:11 NKJV)*

This fifth trumpet is one of the three worst disasters to strike mankind. It is clear that the world is full of evil influences, but the Bible reveals here that God has been holding a tide of evil back. Many people ask why there is so much suffering in the world. The opposite question might be asked: given the state of men's hearts why is there not more suffering in the world? As the world nears its end, God will allow a wave of demonic power to sweep over mankind and the darkness and misery of those who choose a path of sin will worsen.

What will be the sign that this trumpet has sounded? Demons have power to enflame the carnal lusts of sinners, enticing them to indulge in forbidden fruits and excessive pursuit of pleasure. One might expect drug addiction, alcoholism and all manner of substance abuse to abound. There might be increased fascination with the occult and psychic powers. The door to the supernatural might swing open, enticing many people to experiment with supernatural gifts and abilities. Satanic cults and secret societies may multiply. All these things are already evident in Hollywood movies and TV series persuading people to believe they have some supernatural gift.

The good news is that the powers of darkness are unable to afflict those who believe in God who have His seal in their foreheads. Moreover God holds back the activity of evil spirits limiting their ability to torment sinners and not allowing them to kill them. This is an act of mercy designed to awaken people to the folly of choosing evil rather than God. It is an act of grace, intended to humble lawless people and bring them to repentance and faith.

It is also vital not to forget the innumerable multitude revealed in chapter 7. *"But where sin abounded, grace abounded much more."*

(Romans 5:20) As the last days approach and the darkness deepens so also grace will abound and multitudes will be saved.

The Sixth Trumpet: the Call to War

12 The first woe is past. Behold, there are still two woes coming after this.
13 The sixth angel sounded. I heard a voice from the horns of the golden altar which is before God, 14 saying to the sixth angel who had one trumpet, "Free the four angels who are bound at the great river Euphrates!"
15 The four angels were freed who had been prepared for that hour and day and month and year, so that they might kill one third of mankind. 16 The number of the armies of the horsemen was two hundred million. I heard the number of them.

When the sixth trumpet sounded yet another mystery was revealed: that the river Euphrates is a prison for four fearful demonic spirits. We may wonder whether these are spirits that were active in the days of Noah, but no clear explanation is given. The human mind bubbles with inquisitiveness but the answer to our curiosity lies just beyond our reach. If a matter is not revealed in the Bible then it lies beyond our knowledge. The Bible is the record of what we can know about the unseen world, and it is also delineating the limits of that knowledge. Believers do well to admit that there are things we are not meant to know and to accept with thanksgiving the boundaries placed upon our knowledge.

The four angels were released to gather the world to the final war that will reach its climax with the sounding of the seventh and last trumpet and the return of Christ. One third of humanity will die in this war through the activity of these four angels. The army that John saw had 200 million soldiers. Such an army is currently only conceivable from the nation of China.

Chapter Nine

The Strange War Horses of the Invading Army

[17] Thus I saw the horses in the vision, and those who sat on them, having breastplates of fiery red, hyacinth blue, and sulfur yellow; and the heads of lions. Out of their mouths proceed fire, smoke, and sulfur. [18] By these three plagues were one third of mankind killed: by the fire, the smoke, and the sulfur, which proceeded out of their mouths. [19] For the power of the horses is in their mouths, and in their tails. For their tails are like serpents, and have heads, and with them they harm.

This enormous army was riding on horses with heads like lions and fire, smoke and brimstone issuing from their mouths. Death and destruction were dispensed by their mouths and their tails. Their riders wore red, blue and yellow breastplates. The description is vivid and it may be a vision of a modern army with weapons of mass destruction. Perhaps John is using 1st century imagery to describe 21st century technology. This fearsome army seemed to be indomitable, but it was about to meet its match with the return of Christ.

The Stubborn Refusal to Repent

[20] The rest of mankind, who were not killed with these plagues, didn't repent of the works of their hands, that they wouldn't worship demons, and the idols of gold, and of silver, and of brass, and of stone, and of wood; which can neither see, nor hear, nor walk. [21] They didn't repent of their murders, nor of their sorceries, nor of their sexual immorality, nor of their thefts.

Millions will die in this terrible demonically inspired war, but many who survive will continue in their violence, their sorceries and immorality. There is a cure for sin, there is a way out of darkness, depression and evil in all its forms. Repentance is the only step that each individual must take to find that way. These judgments are God's final pleading with a guilty world, and tragically God's call will go largely unheeded.

CHAPTER 10

JOHN'S CALL IS RENEWED

The Renewing of John's Call to Prophesy to the Nations

Another Mighty Angel

Revelation 10:1 *I saw another mighty angel coming down out of the sky, clothed with a cloud. A rainbow was on his head. His face was like the sun, and his feet like pillars of fire. [2] He had in his hand a little open book. He set his right foot on the sea, and his left on the land. [3] He cried with a loud voice, as a lion roars. When he cried, the seven thunders uttered their voices. [4] When the seven thunders sounded, I was about to write; but I heard a voice from the sky saying, "Seal up the things which the seven thunders said, and don't write them."*

John saw a mighty angel with such great majesty and beauty that declared this angel's close union with God. Some have wondered whether the angel might be Jesus Himself. However the little phrase "another mighty angel" holds the key to this question. The Greek word for another is "allos" meaning another of the same kind. The book of Revelation describes the activities of many angels, some with trumpets and some making great declarations. This phrase indicates that this angel is yet another of the same order, firmly placing this angel on the same level as the others.

Chapter Ten

The Bible nowhere invites us to think of Jesus as similar to the angels. Hebrews chapter one highlights the great contrast between Jesus and the angels.

> "Of the angels he says,
> "Who makes his angels winds,
>   and his servants a flame of fire."
> ⁸ But of the Son he says,
> "Your throne, O God, is forever and ever."" (Hebrews 1:7-8)

The New Testament never gives Jesus the title of angel. The Old Testament describes certain moments when an angel is unambiguously described as a manifestation of God (theophany is the technical word). This describes the ability of an angel to so surrender its being to God that it is a manifestation of God. The parents of Samson declared they had seen God after the Angel of the Lord had appeared to them (Judges 13). It is also possible for God to take on any form He wishes. It was a man and not an angel that fought with Jacob at Jabbok (Genesis 32) and Jacob declared that he had seen God. Some have speculated that Melchizedek might have been God appearing in human form. The mechanics of these manifestations of God may be debated at length. But the Bible clearly teaches that God is not a man and Jesus is not an angel. Jesus took on human form in a permanent way, actually becoming a human being.

> "For verily he took not on him the nature of angels; but he took on him the seed of Abraham." (Hebrews 2:16 KJV)

Moreover the description "another mighty angel" is at variance with the almighty power invested in Jesus Christ. Jesus is not just another anything. Nor is He merely mighty. He is almighty God.

The angel roared and John heard seven thunders. He was about to write what he heard but was stopped by the angel. This is not the only time that revelation is given but not to be shared. Paul described a similar experience:

> "how he was caught up into Paradise, and heard unspeakable words, which it is not lawful for a man to utter."
> (2 Corinthians 12:4)

Here John too heard words that he was not permitted to write down.

The Gospel Age Draws to its Close

[5] *The angel whom I saw standing on the sea and on the land lifted up his right hand to the sky,* [6] *and swore by him who lives forever and ever, who created heaven and the things that are in it, the earth and the things that are in it, and the sea and the things that are in it, that there will no longer be delay,* [7] *but in the days of the voice of the seventh angel, when he is about to sound, then the mystery of God is finished, as he declared to his servants, the prophets.*

The mighty angel raised his hand and declared that all delay was now at and end.

> "The Lord is not slow concerning his promise, as some count slowness; but is patient with us, not wishing that any should perish, but that all should come to repentance." (2 Peter 3:9)

God has allowed the day of grace to continue in order that sinners may be saved. This is the only reason that human history is still unfolding. The declaration of the angel is the announcement that this age of grace has ended and the end has come.

The Power of the Little Book

[8] *The voice which I heard from heaven, again speaking with me, said, "Go, take the book which is open in the hand of the angel who stands on the sea and on the land."*

Chapter Ten

⁹I went to the angel, telling him to give me the little book.
He said to me, "Take it, and eat it up. It will make your stomach bitter, but in your mouth it will be as sweet as honey."
¹⁰I took the little book out of the angel's hand, and ate it up. It was as sweet as honey in my mouth. When I had eaten it, my stomach was made bitter. ¹¹They told me, "You must prophesy again over many peoples, nations, languages, and kings."

All the time that the angel was speaking he had been holding a little book. The voice from heaven now commanded John to take the little book. This little book is the Bible, or even perhaps the New Testament. The first century Christians had the books of the Old Testament in Greek (the Septuagint translated around 250 BC). Jews such as the twelve apostles and Paul were familiar with these writings, but the Gentile converts had to learn them from scratch.

The New Testament with its four gospels laying out the life and death of Jesus and His teaching were completed in the course of the sixty years following the cross. Matthew and Mark may have been written within 10 to 15 years after the death and resurrection of Jesus. Luke was probably written around 60 AD and it is possible that John wrote his gospel after he wrote the book of Revelation in 96 AD. Paul's writings (composed between AD 48 and AD 65) were received as scriptures even before the ink was dry:

> *"Regard the patience of our Lord as salvation; even as our beloved brother Paul also, according to the wisdom given to him, wrote to you; ¹⁶as also in all of his letters, speaking in them of these things. In those, there are some things that are hard to understand, which the ignorant and unsettled twist, as they also do to the other Scriptures, to their own destruction." (2 Peter 3:15-16)*

This should not surprise us when we consider the divine approval that rested on the labours of the apostle Paul. The little book, the New

Testament was fresh and new in the hands of God's people in the days of John. The eye-witnesses were dying out, John himself being the last surviving of the original apostles. Now he received the command to take the little book and devour it.

This section is relevant to John for the remainder of his earthly life. It is also a great lesson for all of God's children and especially for those who preach and teach. It explains three principles that should shape our attitude to the Bible in every generation.

1. No one can understand the Bible unless it is given to them. John had to present his firm petition "Give me the little book!" The first act in all Bible reading is to humbly beseech God for comprehension. The Bible is a closed book to the arrogant. It must be read with the heart not just the intellect. The pride of man will find conflicts and contradictions in the Bible and reading with such an attitude will lead to bondage and darkness. Only the grace of God can break open the words to impart revelation of God. The Bible is a foundation stone of God's self-disclosure to the human race. And only through prayer and faith will it yield its mysteries. Many of God's choicest servants read this book on their knees. In the weeks after George Whitefield was converted he devoured the Bible:

   "I began to read the Holy Scriptures on my knees, laying aside all other books, and praying over if possible every line and word. This proved meat indeed and drink indeed to my soul. I daily received fresh life, light, and power from above."[22]"

2. Take it and eat it." The Bible must be devoured. There are many books that inform the mind, imparting information. But the Bible must be absorbed into the heart by an act of faith.

---

[22] George Whitefield, *George Whitefield's Journals,* p 60.Banner of Truth Trust, 1960.

Chapter Ten

"God's Word is supernatural in origin, eternal in duration, inexpressible in valour, infinite in scope, regenerative in power, infallible in authority, universal in application, inspired in totality. Read it through; write it down; pray it in; work it out; pass it on. The Word of God changes a man until he becomes an epistle of God."   Smith Wigglesworth.

John was commanded to take up the Bible and devour it. The human mind is amazing in its power to absorb facts and store them away. Yet the human mind is also capable of losing what was once familiar. We forget so quickly that only what we have absorbed in recent months is at the forefront of our conscious mind. Reading the Bible is like eating food. No one stops eating no matter how well they might have feasted on previous occasions. It is certainly not enough to have once read the whole Bible. Believers and particularly ministers must have a daily, living, dynamic relationship with the Bible.

3. The word will be sweet and then bitter. The reading of the Bible will lead to moments of exquisite delight as the reader bathes his mind and heart in the beautiful fragrant Spirit communicated through the word. But the same word convicts of sin, pride, or unreality and produces inner brokenness and repentance. This may be a bitter experience but it will always lead to life and deeper joy. The Bible was never meant merely to inform, but rather to challenge the will and change the conduct of its readers.

John was given the prophetic promise that he would yet prophesy about many peoples, nations, tongues and kings. In chapter one John received such a revelation of Christ that he lay slain at His feet. Now God speaks to him to continue to devour His word and to have his prophetic ministry deepened and renewed.

CHAPTER 11

THE CHURCH AT THE CLOSE OF THE AGE

The Temple and the 42 Months

Revelation 11:1 *A reed like a rod was given to me. Someone said, "Rise, and measure God's temple, and the altar, and those who worship in it. ² Leave out the court which is outside of the temple, and don't measure it, for it has been given to the nations. They will tread the holy city under foot for forty-two months.*

Will the 3rd Temple be Built?

There are several prophecies that demand either a literal or a symbolic temple to be in existence at the return of Christ but the scriptures do not explicitly state that a literal 3rd temple will be rebuilt. (See Daniel 9:27; Matthew 24:15; and 2 Thessalonians 2:3-4 for verses where a temple is implied).

Belief in a Literal 3rd Temple:

The 1st temple was built by Solomon and finished around 950 BC. It was destroyed by Nebuchadnezzar in 586 BC (2 Chronicles 36:13-19).

Chapter Eleven

The 2nd temple was built by Joshua and Zerubbabel around 500 BC (Ezra 3:8; Zechariah 4:9). This temple was expanded and lavishly embellished by Herod the Great in his reign which lasted 33 years from 37-4 BC. This temple was destroyed by Titus in AD 70 as prophesied by Christ. Jerusalem came under Muslim control in AD 637 and the Dome of the Rock was built on the temple mount around AD 691. Muslims believe that Mohammed was supernaturally transported to Jerusalem by the angel Gabriel and that Mohammed ascended into heaven from Mount Moriah – the temple Mount. For this reason it is the 3rd most holy site of Islam after Mecca and Medina.

The rock around which the Dome is built is generally believed to be the place on which Abraham was led to offer his son as a sacrifice. It is believed to be the site of the Holy of Holies of the 1st and 2nd temple.

Why do many believe that there will be a 3rd temple in the end times? The answer is that Jesus and Paul gave prophecies that imply the existence of a literal temple. Jesus prophesied that the 2nd temple would be destroyed:

> *"His disciples came to him to show him the buildings of the temple. ^{2} But he answered them, "You see all of these things, don't you? Most certainly I tell you, there will not be left here one stone on another, that will not be thrown down."." (Matthew 24:1-2)*

He also prophesied that the abomination of desolation would be set up in "the holy place":

> *"When, therefore, you see the abomination of desolation, which was spoken of through Daniel the prophet, standing in the holy place (let the reader understand)" (Matthew 24:15)*

In 2 Thessalonians Paul says that the Antichrist will sit in the temple of God claiming to be God:

> *"Let no one deceive you by any means; for that Day will not come unless the falling away comes first, and the man of sin is revealed, the son of perdition, ⁴ who opposes and exalts himself above all that is called God or that is worshiped, so that he sits as God in the temple of God, showing himself that he is God."*
> *(2 Thessalonians 2:3-4 NKJV)*

It can be inferred from these verses that a 3rd temple must be built in order for the abomination of desolation to be erected there and for Antichrist to sit there claiming to be God.

Moreover there are plans in place to build a 3rd temple. There is a temple Institute in Jerusalem which has prepared the vestments and utensils and altar for this event. Many Jewish rabbis are praying for the events to take place which will enable their dream to become a reality. There is also no doubt that the temple mount in Jerusalem is the focus of the most heated controversy in the world. Political and religious pressure could easily boil over into war around this very subject.

Could the Temple be Symbolical?

Many believers can see these same prophecies by Jesus and Paul as having their fulfillment in the person of the pope. The popes claimed infallibility and continue to this day to receive worship as believers kiss the pope's hands and feet. Boniface VIII declared:

> *"I am all in all and above all... what therefore can you make of me but God."(Unum Sanctum November 18, 1302).*[23]

The phrase "Antichrist" does not mean opposing Christ but in the place of Christ. The popes then sit in the temple of God, meaning the church - not a 3rd temple in Jerusalem. It is then possible that no 3rd temple will

---

[23] Rev. Peter M.J. Stravinskas, *The Catholic Answer Book 4,* p 219. Our Sunday Visitor Publishing 2003.

be built before the return of Christ and that the abomination of desolation has a fulfilment in the blasphemous claims of men regarding their role in the church. It is easy to imagine a one world religion uniting the 3 religions of the Middle East and seeing the pope, other religious leaders and politicians making blasphemous claims about themselves.

The "Temple" in Revelation 11: 1 is used Figuratively

John was told to measure the temple and the worshippers in it. (This is the only time that John was actively participating in the events placed before him). The word for temple here is the Greek word "naos" meaning the temple building containing the Holy of Holies and the Holy Place where only priests were allowed to enter. But John seems to be using the word temple here figuratively. Here the inner temple is evidently the place of all true worshippers. The outer courts are given over to unbelievers and gentiles. John is here describing the two churches that exist today. The first church believes the Bible and worships God in Spirit and in truth. The second church follows the traditions of men, contradicting the Bible and establishing beliefs and moral standards that are in conflict with the Bible. Many liberal scholars of all the major Christian denominations deny the resurrection, the virgin birth, the atoning death of Christ and the uniqueness of Christ as the only true way to God.

So it is possible that no 3rd temple will be built. It is vital not to become so obsessed with one aspect of Bible prophecy and miss the coming of Christ. Prophecies may be fulfilled in a literal or a symbolic sense and we need to have the humility to recognise that our interpretation may be wrong.

In concluding this section there is one last observation to be made. The dome of the rock is a Muslim prayer shrine and it bears many inscriptions in Arabic around the interior including:

> "God is only One God. Far be it removed from His transcendent majesty that He should have a son."

It is astonishing that such a bold denial of the claim of Christ has stood for so long on the site opposite the Mount of Olives where Jesus made his prophecy about the coming abomination of desolation.

John the author of Revelation wrote in his first epistle:

> "This is the Antichrist, he who denies the Father and the Son.." (1 John 2:22)

Bible prophecy has the astonishing quality that it might be fulfilled in plain sight and yet many of us can so easily miss it.

42 months

This is the first time that the period of 42 months is mentioned in the book of Revelation. It occurs in biblical prophecy in different forms:

1. **A time, times and half a time.**

    Daniel prophesied that Antichrist would be given power to persecute believers for "a time, times and half a time:

    "He shall speak words against the Most High, and shall wear out the saints of the Most High; and he shall think to change the times and the law; and they shall be given into his hand until a time and times and half a time." (Daniel 7:25)

    "I heard the man clothed in linen, who was above the waters of the river, when he held up his right hand and his left hand to heaven, and swore by him who lives forever that it shall be for a time, times, and a half; and when they have finished breaking in pieces the power of the holy people, all these things shall be finished." (Daniel

12:7)

John used the same phrase to indicate the period of time that the church would be persecuted but preserved:

"Two wings of the great eagle were given to the woman, that she might fly into the wilderness to her place, so that she might be nourished for a time, and times, and half a time, from the face of the serpent." (Revelation 12:14)

2. **1260 days (42 x 30).**

   John prophesied that two witnesses would prophesy for this period:

   "And I will give power to my two witnesses, and they will prophesy one thousand two hundred and sixty days, clothed in sackcloth." (Rev 11:3)

   He also prophesied that the church would be persecuted for this same period of time:

   "The woman fled into the wilderness, where she has a place prepared by God, that there they may nourish her one thousand two hundred sixty days." (Revelation 12:6)

3. **42 months**

   John prophesied in Revelation 11:2 that Jerusalem the holy city would be occupied by the Gentiles for this length of time. Revelation 13:5 also says that Antichrist would be given this same time span to rule:

   "A mouth speaking great things and blasphemy was given to him. Authority to make war for forty-two months was given to him." (Revelation 13:5)

This period of time also fits in with Daniel's 70 weeks prophecy, which indicates that the abomination of desolation would be set up in the middle of a final period of seven years:

> "He shall make a firm covenant with many for one week: and in the middle of the week he shall cause the sacrifice and the offering to cease; and on the wing of abominations shall come one who makes desolate; and even to the full end, and that determined, shall wrath be poured out on the desolate." (Daniel 9:27)

From these scriptures we know that the Antichrist will have a period of seven years in which he will have extraordinary power and influence. The last forty two months will be a period of extraordinary persecution: "the Great Tribulation."

The forty two months refers to a specific time of terrible persecution by the Antichrist. This and other prophecies are written in such a manner that believers passing through such deep trials may find comfort in the promise of Christ's return. Many believers in history will have believed they were in the great tribulation. This was true of many who suffered at the hands of Nero, the Spanish Inquisition, Adolf Hitler[24], Mao Tse Tung and Joseph Stalin.

 Almost every generation since the first century has had persecutions somewhere in the world. Moreover there have been many Antichrists, and those living and suffering under their rule would not have been comforted by any assurance that this was not the final Antichrist. The book of Revelation is written in such a way as to bring comfort to all generations of believers.

---

[24] The period of the Holocaust known as the "Final solution" has been dated by some between the end of 1941 and May 1945, a period of approximately 42 months. It was a period of Great Tribulation.

Chapter Eleven

The Two Witnesses

³I will give power to my two witnesses, and they will prophesy one thousand two hundred sixty days, clothed in sackcloth." ⁴These are the two olive trees and the two lamp stands, standing before the Lord of the earth. ⁵If anyone desires to harm them, fire proceeds out of their mouth and devours their enemies. If anyone desires to harm them, he must be killed in this way. ⁶These have the power to shut up the sky, that it may not rain during the days of their prophecy. They have power over the waters, to turn them into blood, and to strike the earth with every plague, as often as they desire. ⁷When they have finished their testimony, the beast that comes up out of the abyss will make war with them, and overcome them, and kill them. ⁸Their dead bodies will be in the street of the great city, which spiritually is called Sodom and Egypt, where also their Lord was crucified. ⁹From among the peoples, tribes, languages, and nations people will look at their dead bodies for three and a half days, and will not allow their dead bodies to be laid in a tomb. ¹⁰Those who dwell on the earth rejoice over them, and they will be glad. They will give gifts to one another, because these two prophets tormented those who dwell on the earth. ¹¹After the three and a half days, the breath of life from God entered into them, and they stood on their feet. Great fear fell on those who saw them. ¹²I heard a loud voice from heaven saying to them, "Come up here!" They went up into heaven in the cloud, and their enemies saw them.

The Law of Moses established that there must be two witnesses for a truth to be established:

> "One witness shall not rise up against a man for any iniquity, or for any sin, in any sin that he sins. At the mouth of two witnesses, or at the mouth of three witnesses, shall a matter be established." (Deuteronomy 19:15)

So once more the great question is: Are the two witnesses two individuals or are they symbols of God's people the church.

Two Individuals?

In the history of Israel there were often two witnesses, for example Moses and Aaron witnessed before Pharaoh of coming disaster for Egypt. Joshua and Caleb witnessed to their generation that God was able to fulfill His promises. Elijah and Elisha witnessed to Ahab and the northern kingdom of Israel that God was displeased with the nation. Joshua and Zerubbabel witnessed that God would rebuild and establish Jerusalem. Jesus sent the disciples out two by two (Luke 10:1).

The description in this chapter contains details that suggest a literal interpretation. They are killed and their bodies lie in the streets of Jerusalem for 3½ days. It is almost impossible to interpret this symbolically. Nevertheless there are details which are equally difficult to interpret literally. For example fire proceeds from their mouths to kill their enemies. It was prophesied of Jesus:

> *"but with righteousness he will judge the poor,*
> *and decide with equity for the humble of the earth.*
> *He will strike the earth with the rod of his mouth;*
> *and with the breath of his lips he will kill the wicked.."*
> *(Isaiah 11:4)*

This is an example of a symbolic description of the power of Jesus' ministry to convict of sin and bring fierce condemnation to those who reject Him. In Matthew 23 Jesus pronounced 7 woes on the scribes and Pharisees and His words would have been as fire to the hearers.

As difficult as it may be to imagine the literal fulfillment of these prophecies there is no reason to reject a literal. The description of the ministry of these witnesses resembles that of Moses and Elijah. Moses turned the waters of the Nile to blood (Exodus 7:20) and Elijah prayed that it would not rain for three and a half years or 42 months (1 Kings 17:1; James 5:17). Many have speculated that God will send a reincarnation of these two individuals but this has no biblical foundation. In Matthew 17:11-13 Jesus confirmed that John the Baptist was the fulfilment of the prophecy that God would send Elijah before the coming of Messiah but he was not a reincarnation of Elijah. John flatly denied that he was Elijah (John 1:21). In Luke 1:17 the angel of the Lord prophesied that John would come in the spirit and power of Elijah, not that he would be a reincarnation of the same person.

The Symbolic Significance of the 2 Witnesses:

The Jew and the Gentile: God has established the identity of the Messiah through the witness of Jews by the prophets and the 12 apostles but also through Gentiles. Job was a Gentile and witnessed of his assurance in the coming bodily resurrection (Job 19:25-27). God has one people not two, but the Bible recognizes that the church is made up of Jews and Gentiles. Joshua was of the tribe of Ephraim (Numbers 13:8) and Caleb was of the tribe of Judah (Numbers 13:6) but Caleb was not born of that tribe. He was the son of Jephunneh the Kenizzite (Numbers 32:12). The Kenizzites were one of the nations that lived in the land of Canaan before the conquest by Joshua (Genesis 15:19). So Caleb was a Gentile converted to faith in the God of Israel. There were many such converts in Israel including Ruth the Moabitess, Rahab from Jericho, Uriah the Hittite and Obed Edom the Gittite. The name Caleb means "dog."[25] So when Joshua and Caleb entered the land of Canaan it was an Israelite and a Gentile walking side by side as one. The same is true of the church. The early church was 100% Jewish until Gentiles began to be added to the church in Acts 10 (Cornelius) and Acts 11:19-22 (Greeks). Since then the church has been made up of Jews and Gentiles witnessing to the truth that Jesus is the Messiah.

---

[25] Strong's concordance 03612. The word Caleb has two meanings and Young's concordance gives the other definition as "bold, impetuous." The name is made up of two words meaning literally "whole hearted."

If the two witnesses symbolise the church at the end of the age then these are her identifying characteristics:

1. The two witnesses are also prophets and the end-times church will be prophetic, warning of imminent judgment and uncovering hidden works of darkness (verse 3).
2. The two witnesses have power in prayer (verse 6).
3. They are clothed in sackcloth (verse 3). The two witnesses are filled with grief at the state of the world and are interceding in anguish for a lost and unrepentant world.
4. They are full of faith and power to do great signs and wonders as Moses and Elijah (verse 6).
5. They suffer terrible persecution and are finally killed (verse 7).
6. They are always rising from the ashes – the church cannot be defeated but grows fastest and strongest when persecuted (verse 11).

It is astonishing to see the resilience of the church in times of persecution and apparent reversal. Communist China has tried to stamp out Christianity only to find that it has multiplied more than anywhere else in history.

> "At least five times, therefore … the Faith has to all appearance gone to the dogs. In each of these five cases it was the dog that died." G.K. Chesterton[26]

The church of the last days will be like the church of the first century with its boldness, evangelical zeal, prophetic and supernatural power and willingness to suffer, supremely confident in the Resurrection.

The two witnesses will fulfill their ministry in Jerusalem the Holy City. Here John is told that the true nature of this city is more like Sodom and

---

[26] G.K. Chesterton, *The Everlasting Man, part 2 chapter 6.* Hodder & Stoughton, London 1925.

Egypt, with their sexual immorality and their pagan idolatry. The clash between the church and the world is a growing reality as the nations descend into moral chaos, spiritual darkness and confusion.

The Final Earthquake

[13] In that day there was a great earthquake, and a tenth of the city fell. Seven thousand people were killed in the earthquake, and the rest were terrified, and gave glory to the God of heaven. [14] The second woe is past. Behold, the third woe comes quickly.

The period of time introduced by the sixth trumpet is concluded by a great earthquake that destroys one tenth of Jerusalem. The number of seven thousand that die in that earthquake seems quite small compared to the awful calamities that strike the earth on earlier occasions. Perhaps it is an indication of the small number of survivors from the previous six trumpets and especially the sixth trumpet and the war of Armageddon.

The Last Trumpet[27]

[15] The seventh angel sounded, and great voices in heaven followed, saying, "The kingdom of the world has become the Kingdom of our Lord, and of his Christ. He will reign forever and ever!"
[16] The twenty-four elders, who sit on their thrones before God's throne, fell on their faces and worshiped God, [17] saying: "We give you thanks, Lord God, the Almighty, the one who is and who was; because you have taken your great power, and reigned. [18] The nations were angry, and your wrath came, as did the time for the dead to be judged, and to give your bondservants the prophets, their reward, as well as to the saints,

---

[27] The word "trumpet" does not appear in most English translations after Revelation 9:14. The word "sounded" however is more literally translated "trumpeted" being the verb form "salpizo" of the noun "salpigx" meaning "trumpet."

and those who fear your name, to the small and the great; and to destroy those who destroy the earth."

[19] *God's temple that is in heaven was opened, and the ark of the Lord's covenant was seen in his temple. Lightnings, sounds, thunders, an earthquake, and great hail followed.*

The sounding of the last trumpet is the herald of the return of Christ. This is the final woe of the last three most awful calamities to strike the earth. Why is the return of Christ described as a woe? Because it will be a terrible act of judgment on the human race. As when God shut the door of the ark, it signals the end of the age of mankind's freedom to rebel against God and to reject righteousness. For those who love Jesus, His return is the sweetest day, but to those who love and practice evil it is a day of darkness and uncovering of secret sins practiced in dark corners. Even for those who love God there are aspects of the great and terrible day of the Lord which should cause all to tremble. But the day of the Lord is a day of deepest darkness to those who practice evil.

> *""Woe to you who desire the day of Yahweh!*
> *Why do you long for the day of Yahweh?*
> *It is darkness,*
> *and not light.*
> [19] *As if a man fled from a lion,*
> *and a bear met him;*
> *Or he went into the house and leaned his hand on the wall,*
> *and a snake bit him.*
> [20] *Won't the day of Yahweh be darkness, and not light?*
> *Even very dark, and no brightness in it? (Amos 5:18-20)*

The last trumpet will signal the resurrection of the righteous to eternal life:

> *"Behold, I tell you a mystery. We will not all sleep, but we will all be changed, in a moment, in the twinkling of an eye, at the last trumpet. For the trumpet will sound, and the dead will be raised incorruptible, and we will be changed." (1 Corinthians 15:51-52)*

Chapter Eleven

The last trumpet is also the signal for the gathering of believers from all corners of the earth often called "the rapture":

> *"He will send out his angels with a great sound of a trumpet, and they will gather together his chosen ones from the four winds, from one end of the sky to the other." (Matthew 24:31)*

> *"For the Lord himself will descend from heaven with a shout, with the voice of the archangel, and with God's trumpet. The dead in Christ will rise first, [17] then we who are alive, who are left, will be caught up together with them in the clouds, to meet the Lord in the air. So we will be with the Lord forever." (1 Thessalonians 4:16-17).*

The sounding of the seventh trumpet signals the beginning of the millennial reign of Christ which will be described in chapter 20 in more detail. John heard the cry of the voices in heaven that declare that the kingdoms of this world have become the kingdoms of our Lord and of His Christ. John also heard the declaration that the time of general resurrection has come and the Day of Judgment. (Revelation 20 will later indicate a thousand year separation between the resurrection of the just and the unjust). The history of the world has drawn to a close and the timeline of Revelation ends with the proclamation of the eternal reign of Christ.

CHAPTER 12

GOD'S TRIUMPHANT PEOPLE

The Vision of God's Triumphant People.

The Woman Bringing Forth the Son

Revelation 12:1 *A great sign was seen in heaven: a woman clothed with the sun, and the moon under her feet, and on her head a crown of twelve stars. ² She was with child. She cried out in pain, laboring to give birth. ³ Another sign was seen in heaven. Behold, a great red dragon, having seven heads and ten horns, and on his heads seven crowns. ⁴ His tail drew one third of the stars of the sky, and threw them to the earth. The dragon stood before the woman who was about to give birth, so that when she gave birth he might devour her child. ⁵ She gave birth to a son, a male child, who is to rule all the nations with a rod of iron. Her child was caught up to God, and to his throne.*

The timeline of Revelation has ended in chapter 11 and now John is taken to see the great powers that shape the history of the world in the last days. He first sees the people of God symbolised by a woman bringing forth a male child.

Chapter Twelve

In these phrases the purpose of the ages is revealed; the purpose of God's dealings with the human race and the calling and destiny of God's people in every age. This calling is that they offer up themselves to God to be indwelt by His Holy Spirit and to be the body of Christ in the earth. God created humanity in the image of God to rule in the earth (Genesis 1:26) but tragically the human race disobeyed and became a manifestation of the kingdom of darkness. God then set about redeeming humanity and fulfilling the original plan for their creation. There are four great steps in the unfolding of this mystery.

1. God called Israel with the purpose that they would bring the Messiah into the world. The Messiah was promised to Adam and Eve in the Garden of Eden immediately after their fall. The promised line passed through Seth, Noah, Shem, Abraham, Isaac and Jacob. Then the Law of Moses shaped Israel through righteousness, preparing a people praying and longing for Messiah to come.

2. The tabernacle was a physical demonstration of God's purpose to make the nation to be a body for God to live in.
   "And let them make Me a sanctuary, that I may dwell among them." (Exodus 25:8)
   The tent or tabernacle had badger skins and supporting pillars like bones and took approximately 9 months to build from the giving of the law at Sinai in the 3rd month of the first year (Exodus 19:1) to the first day of the first month of the second year (Exodus 40:1-2).

3. God's purpose was fulfilled literally in the person of Mary the mother of Jesus. Mary had been shaped by the law and brought to righteousness and beautiful surrender to the Holy Spirit.
   "The Holy Spirit will come upon you, and the power of the Highest will overshadow you; therefore, also, that Holy One who is to be born will be called the Son of God. (Luke 1:35)
   "The word became flesh and dwelt – literally tabernacled - amongst us." John 1:14.

4. The teaching of Jesus prepared Israel to receive the Holy Spirit and to fulfil their destiny as the church - the body of Messiah. The New Covenant was made with the house of Israel. Acts 2 is a very Jewish chapter and the first church was made up of Jews including the mother of Jesus. Mary allowed Christ to be formed in her womb physically and then later received the Holy Spirit to form Christ in her personality. The indwelling of Messiah is the final fulfilment of this great plan: *"Christ in you the hope of glory."* Colossians 1:27.

Many argue whether the woman is Israel or the church, missing the point that faithful Israel (Mary, the apostles, Paul, Barnabas etc.) were the first members of the church. The Gentiles were not included immediately in order to emphasize this point that the Gentiles were made partakers of the great calling of God for the people of Israel. God's purpose for the Jews is still unchanged: that they will receive Jesus as their Messiah and become a dwelling place of God by the Holy Spirit as on the day of Pentecost.

What is God's purpose for each believer? It is to be a home for God, the continuation of the incarnation, a vessel in which Christ is to be formed in His full authority and maturity. The cross, the resurrection, the outpouring of the Holy Spirit and the teaching of the apostles are all to present every believer perfect and mature in Christ Jesus. God wants His man child Christ to be formed in full stature in every individual and every church corporately.

The Dragon

Satan is a fierce enemy of the will of God especially as it relates to the fulfillment of this plan. Satan seeks to keep believers as spiritual babies. He opposes the manifestation of God in Christ. He attempted to blot out the seed of David through the wickedness of Athaliah (2 Kings 11:1). Satan tried to destroy the infant Jesus through the malice of Herod (Matthew 2:16). The dragon is the implacable enemy of the church and seeks to stop the church ruling in spiritual power through the indwelling Christ.

The church first appeared as a great wonder in heaven on the day of Pentecost, when the believers were caught up into heavenly places through the baptism with the Holy Spirit. This signalled the beginning of intense warfare.

The Woman and Warfare in the Heavens

[6] The woman fled into the wilderness, where she has a place prepared by God, that there they may nourish her one thousand two hundred sixty days.
[7] There was war in the heavens. Michael and his angels made war on the dragon. The dragon and his angels made war. [8] They didn't prevail, neither was a place found for him any more in heaven. [9] The great dragon was thrown down, the old serpent, he who is called the devil and Satan, the deceiver of the whole world. He was thrown down to the earth, and his angels were thrown down with him. [10] I heard a loud voice in heaven, saying, "Now the salvation, the power, and the Kingdom of our God, and the authority of his Christ has come; for the accuser of our brothers has been thrown down, who accuses them before our God day and night.

The church, the bride of Christ, had to flee from the face of the serpent and she must do this by flying on the wings of an eagle (verse 14). Just as Christ overcame the devil in the wilderness, so also believers must do battle and overcome Satan. All believers have a place prepared by God for them, before His throne. This place is discovered by the rigours of self-denial in a desolate place. When we first enter the wilderness our flesh cries out for the pleasures of the world, for the stimulating tastes and sounds of entertainment, of good food, of pleasant music. But as we abide in the abstinence imposed by wilderness life our spiritual senses are awakened and we become more conscious of God and enjoy His word. We discover that we live by His word. The wilderness begins to blossom and flourish as the garden of the Lord, and we realise that we were duped by the stimulation of our senses. The wilderness is death to the outward man, but a door of life to the inward man. Many of God's choicest servants found their deepest encounters with God in solitary confinement in prison. The apostles, Madame Guyon, Corrie Ten Boom, Richard Wurmbrand and brother Yun are all examples of suffering saints who demonstrate how negatives become positive.

Warfare in the heavens is the reality behind the flow of history. These verses describe the great moment when Satan was expelled from heaven by the victory of Calvary. Jesus declared the victory of Calvary as follows:

> "Now is the judgment of this world. Now the prince of this world will be cast out." (John 12:31)

The spiritual world changed when Jesus died on the cross:

> "Having disarmed principalities and powers, He made a public spectacle of them, triumphing over them in it." (Col. 2:15 NKJV)

On the cross Jesus destroyed Satan:

> "Since then the children have shared in flesh and blood, he also himself in the same way partook of the same, that through death he might bring to nothing him who had the power of death, that is, the devil, [15] and might deliver all of them who through fear of death were all their lifetime subject to bondage." (Hebrews 2:14-15)

That Satan was destroyed at Calvary does not mean he ceased to exist. It refers to the fact that the devil was cast out of heaven and lost his power to accuse believers before the throne of God. This victory was the triumph of Calvary and ushered in the gospel age: "*Now is come salvation*" (verse 10).

Chapter Twelve

The Secret of an Overcoming Life

¹¹ They overcame him because of the Lamb's blood, and because of the word of their testimony. They didn't love their life, even to death. ¹² Therefore rejoice, heavens, and you who dwell in them. Woe to the earth and to the sea, because the devil has gone down to you, having great wrath, knowing that he has but a short time."
¹³ When the dragon saw that he was thrown down to the earth, he persecuted the woman who gave birth to the male child. ¹⁴ Two wings of the great eagle were given to the woman, that she might fly into the wilderness to her place, so that she might be nourished for a time, and times, and half a time, from the face of the serpent. ¹⁵ The serpent spewed water out of his mouth after the woman like a river, that he might cause her to be carried away by the stream. ¹⁶ The earth helped the woman, and the earth opened its mouth and swallowed up the river which the dragon spewed out of his mouth. ¹⁷ The dragon grew angry with the woman, and went away to make war with the rest of her offspring, who keep God's commandments and hold Jesus' testimony.

Four great secrets of an overcoming life are given in this section:

1. **The blood of the Lamb**
   Jesus said that believers must drink His blood not just believe in it:
   "Then Jesus said to them, "Most assuredly, I say to you, unless you eat the flesh of the Son of Man and drink His blood, you have no life in you." (John 6:53 NKJV)
   Jesus poured out His blood in a most awful death so that sinners might be forgiven and cleansed. The blood has power because it is applied to our inward life. It is God's bleaching agent to remove the most stubborn stains of sin from our conduct. It is also God's dye to colour our lives with His character. The blood removes sin and imparts love and holiness. The blood is God's own being, His essence, imparted to His beloved people on Calvary. In the communion we drink His blood but that is just a

picture of the reality of receiving the essential life of God as we drink His Spirit and commune with Him.

2. **The word of their testimony**
   Believers have an inner testimony and it is vital that we speak boldly what we know in our hearts by the Holy Spirit. Satan would intimidate believers to accept his lies. Many have lived for years with low self-esteem, even self-hatred in some cases. Others have lived in pride and hardness before their conversion. Satan continues to condemn believers and reminds them of their sins. But we are to boldly declare that we are justified, declared righteous by faith. Once Christ is in us we must put off the old man and put on the new. We must confidently confess that we are beloved children of God no matter what pain and sufferings we may have to endure.

3. **They loved not their lives unto death**
   All victories in spiritual life are rooted in embracing death to self. This is the lesson of the wilderness where we lose all the comforts that pamper our self-life. Embracing the cross is the foundation of discipleship. We must deny ourselves, take up our cross and follow Christ. This ruggedly unselfish life-style is essential if we are to overcome the temptations of the enemy and live a life of powerful effective witness. It is not embracing an austere or ascetic lifestyle; it is a radical transfer of ownership:
   "I as a child of God belong to heaven and to God. It is not a question of giving up sin but of giving up my right to myself, my natural independence and my self-will. This is where the battle has to be fought."   Oswald Chambers.

4. **Two wings of a great eagle**
   God has a special place prepared in the Spirit for His people to escape and be nourished from the face of the enemy. But this place can only be reached on the wings of an eagle.

Chapter Twelve

"But those who wait on the LORD Shall renew their strength; They shall mount up with wings like eagles, They shall run and not be weary, They shall walk and not faint." (Isaiah 40:31 NKJV)

This place cannot be reached by study, nor by force of striving or intellect. It can only be reached by unfolding the wings of faith and worship and waiting on the Lord. The discipline of waiting on the Lord is the art of stilling the clamour and chatter of our minds till we become conscious of the divine presence in our hearts. The touch of the Holy Spirit awakens our souls to soar and sing. The more we are conscious of God in His perfect beauty and splendor, the more our hearts rise in confidence to His throne. Believers may be caged in prisons, but no-one can stop believers from rising above every situation and escaping to a secret place, where we eat secret food that the world knows nothing of. The eagle does not flutter like a butterfly with fragile wings, nor does it strain like a bee with tiny wings that keep it aloft by intense beating. The eagle has wide wings that catch the upward thermals of rising air and enable it to fly with effortless ease. The eagle cannot travel by walking, it must fly, and so it is with Christians. We must spread our wings of faith and catch the ministry of the Spirit. We must march to a different drum beat and so escape the floods of evil that proceed from the mouth of the dragon.

The Earth Helps the Bride

It is rare that the purposes of God find help from the governments of this world but God can move kings, presidents and prime ministers to do His will. God used Cyrus to bring the Jews back to their land after the Babylonian captivity. He used the British government by prompting Prime Minister Lloyd George and foreign minister Balfour to issue the Balfour declaration triggering the return of the Jews and the creation of the state of Israel in 1948. God has used the American government to stand up to foreign aggression against the state of Israel, particularly in the 1973 Yom Kippur war. God has used pressure from western democracies to periodically and temporarily improve freedom of religion in many countries such as China and Russia. Many persecuted pastors have been freed from prison through the diplomacy and the threat of economic sanctions from American and other western governments,

The devil was cast down to the earth by the victory of Calvary. Believers on the contrary have escaped the earth to live in heavenly places in Christ Jesus:

> *"God has raised us up with him, and made us to sit with him in the heavenly places in Christ Jesus." (Ephesians 2:6)*

Those who do not know Christ are cut off from the supply of strength and comfort given to those who rise above the darkness on eagles wings.

The Time, Times and Half a Time

Once more this chapter refers to the three and a half years at the end of the age, which must be taken to be a literal period of intense persecution, and yet this chapter would have given strength and courage to all believers in history. The chapter covers a vast period from the victory of the cross to the return of Christ. It tells of a cosmic battle that rages against the forming of the full stature of Christ in each of us. This conflict requires believers in all ages to rise up and use the weapons of our warfare and overcome the powers of darkness, triumphing with those brave Christians of past ages who have laid down their lives in fearless testimony of the power of Jesus to save to the uttermost.

CHAPTER 13

THE BEAST AND THE FALSE PROPHET

The First Beast: the Antichrist

Revelation 13:1 *Then I stood on the sand of the sea. I saw a beast coming up out of the sea, having ten horns and seven heads. On his horns were ten crowns, and on his heads, blasphemous names. ² The beast which I saw was like a leopard, and his feet were like those of a bear, and his mouth like the mouth of a lion. The dragon gave him his power, his throne, and great authority. ³ One of his heads looked like it had been wounded fatally. His fatal wound was healed, and the whole earth marveled at the beast. ⁴ They worshiped the dragon, because he gave his authority to the beast, and they worshiped the beast, saying, "Who is like the beast? Who is able to make war with him?" ⁵ A mouth speaking great things and blasphemy was given to him. Authority to make war for forty-two months was given to him. ⁶ He opened his mouth for blasphemy against God, to blaspheme his name, and his dwelling, those who dwell in heaven. ⁷ It was given to him to make war with the saints, and to overcome them. Authority over every tribe, people, language, and nation was given to him. ⁸ All who dwell on the earth will worship him, everyone whose name has not been written from the foundation of the world in the book of life of the Lamb who has been killed. ⁹ If anyone has an ear, let him hear. ¹⁰ If anyone is to go into* *captivity, he will go into captivity. If anyone is to be killed with the sword, he must be killed. Here is the endurance and the faith of the saints.*

12 Facets of the Beast Revealed in Revelation Chapter 13

John now saw the Antichrist, the focus of evil in the last days and the ruler of a world empire. Here are twelve facets about him that are revealed in this chapter:

1. He will rise out of the sea, which represents humanity agitated perhaps by revolution or economic woes (as in Russia and Germany in the first part of the 20th century) Rev 13:1.
2. He has seven heads and ten horns and ten diadems (unmerited crowns not victors' crowns). Antichrist will be the head of a confederation of nations Rev 13:1.
3. He receives power from the most evil source of all – the dragon Rev 13:4. In Matt 4:9 Satan offered political power to Jesus if He would bow to Satan. Antichrist will bow to Satan. Many politicians unconsciously bow to Satan when they shed blood to obtain or keep political power. Some bribe their way to high office and unconsciously cooperate with the powers of darkness. A small number have consciously invoked occult powers to aid their rise. Antichrist will probably operate all these levers of power offered him by Satan.
4. The Antichrist will be popular to the point of adulation: Rev 13:4 – he is worshipped by the whole world.
5. He will be blasphemous – Rev 13:5 speaking evil lies about God and His people.
6. He will have military supremacy – Rev 13:4 so that no-one can make war with him.
7. He will persecute and kill Christians –Rev 13:7.
8. He will be a combination of former beasts (Antichrists) and will be an animal part leopard, part bear and part lion Rev 13:2. In Daniel chapter 7 the lion represents Babylon (modern day Iraq), the bear

represents Persia (modern day Iran) and the leopard represents Greece.
9. He will suffer an assassination attempt but will survive as if by a miracle. This may mean an attempt on his life or a political setback, followed by a revival of his fortunes Rev 13:3.
10. His end is inevitable – he will be destroyed. Rev 13:10 assures believers that all who kill with the sword must themselves die by the sword.
11. He shall rule unopposed for 42 months: Rev 13:5.
12. He shall be the supreme ruler of the whole world holding all peoples, tongues and nations in thrall of him Rev 13:7.

10 Aspects of the Antichrist Revealed in other Parts of the Bible

The coming of the Antichrist is prophesied in other Bible passages and here are 10 aspects that we learn:

1. The Antichrist will be the culmination of a series of Antichrists with similar characteristics. *"Little children, these are the end times, and as you heard that the Antichrist is coming, even now many antichrists have arisen. By this we know that it is the final hour."* (1 John 2:18)

2. The Antichrist will propagate religious beliefs that contradict foundational Christian teaching. He will deny the trinity: *"Who is the liar but he who denies that Jesus is the Christ? This is the Antichrist, he who denies the Father and the Son."* (1 John 2:22)
He will deny the incarnation: *"And every spirit who doesn't confess that Jesus Christ has come in the flesh is not of God, and this is the spirit of the Antichrist, of whom you have heard that it comes. Now it is in the world already."* (1 John 4:3)
"For many deceivers have gone out into the world, those who don't confess that Jesus Christ came in the flesh. This is the deceiver and the Antichrist." (2 John 1:7)

There are many liberal theologians, religions and sects that deny the teachings of the New Testament. Antichrist will arise with a religious faith that is in conflict with the claims of Christ and the teaching of the Bible.

3. The religious aspect of the Antichrist is revealed in his title "The son of perdition" (2 Thessalonians 2:3 KJV) which he shares with the apostle Judas. He is also called "The lawless one" (2 Thessalonians 2:8) indicating his immoral behavior which he also shared with Judas who stole regularly from the common purse of the apostles (John 12:6) and he finally betrayed Jesus for money.

4. His character is the opposite of Jesus Christ. Jesus humbled Himself while Antichrist will exalt himself (Daniel 11:37). Christ obeyed the will of the Father while Antichrist will follow his own will (Daniel 11:36). Christ cleansed the temple (Mark 11:15-16) while Antichrist will defile the temple (Daniel 9:27). Christ came from heaven (John 3:13) while the Antichrist rises from the pit (Revelation 11:7).

5. Antichrist will be a prince from the Roman Empire (Daniel 9:26).

6. He will be part of a large confederation of nations but shall subdue three rulers under his power (Daniel 7:8).

7. He shall change his religion Daniel 11:37-39. He will honour the god of fortresses and a foreign god.

8. He shall not be drawn to women and may be unmarried or homosexual (Daniel 11:37).

9. He shall change laws and times (Daniel 7:25). This has been attempted by several governments for example during the French Revolution.[28]

10. Antichrist will make war with Christ (Revelation 19:19) but shall be immediately cast into the lake of fire prior to the day of judgement (Revelation 20:20) where he will be tormented forever with the devil (Revelation 20:10).

The Trinity of Evil: The Dragon, the Antichrist and the False Prophet

The activity of Satan in the last days is a blasphemous parody of the Trinity and is the culmination of his desire to be like the Most High (Isaiah 14:14).

- The followers of Jesus have His name in their foreheads (Revelation 14:1) as do the followers of the beast.
- The beast has a miraculous recovery mimicking the resurrection (Revelation 13:3).
- The false prophet performs signs through the power of Satan (the dragon) to authenticate the beast and glorify him, just as the Holy Spirit glorifies Christ. *"The coming of the lawless one is according to the working of Satan with all power and signs and lying wonders." (2 Thessalonians 2:9)*
- The Antichrist has his appearing or "Parousia" in Greek (2 Thessalonians 2:9). This is the same word used for the second coming of Christ (2 Thessalonians 2:1,8).

This trinity of evil will seek to deceive the whole world and usurp the place belonging to Jesus the Son of God.

---

[28] The French Republican calendar was created and implemented during the French Revolution, and used by the French government for some 12 years from late 1793 to 1805. The revolutionary calendar was designed to remove all religious and royalist references from the calendar, and was part of a larger attempt at decimalisation in France (e.g. a ten day week, a ten hour day).

Three Examples of Antichrists from History

While we may find it difficult to imagine such a ruler in the future, we can understand what kind of person he will be by looking at politicians in history who have been Antichrists.

1. Antiochus Epiphanes: In 167 BC, Antiochus Epiphanes exalted himself above God and stopped the daily sacrifices in the temple in Jerusalem. Antiochus ordered the public burning of the Torah in Israel and forbade circumcision and Sabbath observance. He offered pigs on the altar in Jerusalem, dedicating it to the Greek god Zeus. He had athletes compete naked in the Greek tradition in Jerusalem. He massacred some 40,000 Jews in Judea, while another 40,000 were sold into slavery. The Maccabeus family rebelled and the temple was cleansed in 164 BC, exactly 42 months after the desecration occurred. Daniel prophesied this describing the desecration as follows:

"Then they shall take away the continual burnt offering, and they shall set up the abomination that makes desolate." (Daniel 11:31)

Daniel also prophesied that Antiochus would die suddenly but not by human means (Daniel 11:25). Antiochus died suddenly of disease in BC 164.

2. Nero: AD 54 to 68. Nero like Caesar Augustus was worshipped as God during his lifetime. Nero was the first political persecutor of Christians and the murderer of the apostles Peter and Paul. Early Christians believed that Nero was the Antichrist. When transliterated into Hebrew, the letters of Nero's name add up to 666.[29] Nero blamed the Christians for the fire that destroyed Rome

---

[29] R.C. Sproul, *The Last Days According To Jesus*, p. 188, Baker Books, 1998.

in AD 64 and brutally murdered thousands. The early church was convinced that he was the Antichrist.[30]

Nero died in AD 68 and it was another Roman Emperor (Vespasian) who conquered Jerusalem in AD 70, destroying the temple and defiling the Holy Places by raising the idolatrous Roman standards in the ruins.

3. Adolf Hitler: 1933-45. Hitler rose to power on a right wing platform promising to rid Germany of the Jews, whom he blamed for all the woes of the world. He and his followers set about exterminating the Jews in concentration camps. Six million died, but far from destroying the Jews he triggered a mass immigration of Jews into the British protectorate of Palestine. On May 1948 the state of Israel was proclaimed and in 1967 Jerusalem was taken during the Six Day War and from that time Israel has proclaimed Jerusalem as its capital. Hitler certainly presided over a period of Great Tribulation for Jews and Christians. Hitler fulfilled many of the prophecies of Antichrist, in that he did not love women and was not married till the day of his death. But Hitler never claimed to be God and never sat in a temple either figuratively or literally even though his followers gave him worship which he actively encouraged. It is not hard to believe that Hitler was demon possessed and that many of his outbursts revealed an irrational dark side to his character.[31]

There are many in history who abused power and may be described as Antichrists. Joseph Stalin and Mao Tse Tung both presided over atheist governments which slaughtered millions. Although much time could be taken exploring these many monsters of history, this small selection gives an understanding of how awful the final Great Tribulation will be.

---

[30] In one textual variation the number 666 is replaced with the number 616 which was the number value of Nero's name in Latin. Some believe that this was deliberate for the Latin readers of the book of Revelation so they would understand that the number was referring to Nero.

[31] Roger Manvell and Heinrich Fraenkel, *Hitler, The Man And The Myth*, p.151. Grafton Books, 1978.

It may be assumed that millions of believers and Jews will die at the hands of the awful dictator who will hold absolute power at the end of this age of history. He will have a religious dimension to his megalomania and will combine religious delusion with fanatical political and military ambitions.

The Second Beast: the False Prophet

[11] I saw another beast coming up out of the earth. He had two horns like a lamb, and he spoke like a dragon. [12] He exercises all the authority of the first beast in his presence. He makes the earth and those who dwell in it to worship the first beast, whose fatal wound was healed. [13] He performs great signs, even making fire come down out of the sky to the earth in the sight of people. [14] He deceives my own people who dwell on the earth because of the signs he was granted to do in front of the beast; saying to those who dwell on the earth, that they should make an image to the beast who had the sword wound and lived. [15] It was given to him to give breath to it, to the image of the beast, that the image of the beast should both speak, and cause as many as wouldn't worship the image of the beast to be killed. [16] He causes all, the small and the great, the rich and the poor, and the free and the slave, to be given marks on their right hands, or on their foreheads; [17] and that no one would be able to buy or to sell, unless he has that mark, the name of the beast or the number of his name. [18] Here is wisdom. He who has understanding, let him calculate the number of the beast, for it is the number of a man. His number is 666.

The second beast is the political ally of the Antichrist. He is his propaganda minister presenting a lamb's countenance but he will have the voice and heart of the dragon. Joseph Goebbels was Hitler's minister of propaganda charged with creating enthusiastic support for Hitler and his policies. Many of these were evil, but the presentation in cinemas across Germany was of the creation of an Aryan paradise. Smiling children and happy families were the benign face of an evil plan to exterminate thousands of children and destroy Jewish families.

Chapter Thirteen

Here are 10 things we learn about the second beast:

1. He is inspired by the power of Satan – he has the voice of the dragon (Rev 13:11).
2. He represents the first beast seeking to inspire worship of the Antichrist.
3. He has supernatural power at this disposal, causing fire to come down from heaven.
4. He motivates the followers of Antichrist to make an image of him. He then makes the image speak and breathe. Some have wondered if this is a reference to television and other modern forms of communication. This would lack the supernatural power implied in these verses.
5. He leads a program of religious persecution causing those who refuse to worship the Antichrist to be killed.
6. He enforces economic dictatorship. He forces all who worship the beast to receive a mark in their hand and in their forehead. Some have assumed this to mean a chip implant but this may not be the meaning of these verses. Such an interpretation deflects the reader from the moral issues that are raised. Whether or not it is linked to a chip implant, the central issue is the giving of worship to the Antichrist, worship that belongs exclusively to Christ. When politicians and businessmen lie or practice corruption there will be a change in their appearance (the forehead) and their activities (the hand). Just as one can see a difference in the countenance of believers (who have the Father's name inscribed in their foreheads Rev 14:1) so too the countenance of those who bow to Satan's demands through the Antichrist receive a change in their face and their practice.
7. 666 – the number of the Antichrist. This number has also many interpretations some suggesting that it is the 18 digit bar code used to identify goods. Many theories will come and go and so rather than speculating it is sufficient at this point to indicate some specific facts about this number:

- Six is the number of man because Adam was created on the sixth day. 3 is the number of divinity, the Trinity. 666 represents man trying to take the place of deity. This is clearly established in scriptures such as
  "He who opposes and exalts himself against all that is called God or that is worshiped; so that he sits as God in the temple of God, setting himself up as God.. (2 Thessalonians 2:4)
- 666 is mentioned in only one other place in the Bible:
  "Now the weight of gold that came to Solomon in one year was six hundred and sixty-six talents of gold," (2 Chronicles 9:13)
  The Greek word for wealth "euphoria" has a number value of 666 in the Greek language. The number of the beast represents the uncontrolled greed and lust that led to Solomon's downfall.
- The 6th letter of the Hebrew Alphabet "w" or "vav" has a number value of 6. Every time a person writes "www" to enter a website, they are writing the number 666. The letters www are an abbreviation for world wide web. Satan's plan is to unite the nations in rebellion against God. This was his stratagem in the tower of Babel. The internet is an essential part of the increasing globalisation and uniting of the human race. This does not mean that the internet is intrinsically evil. It is a tool that may be used for good or evil, but it is vital to grasp the underlying plan of Satan to build another tower of Babel. (This will be explored further in chapters 17 and 18).
- It has already been noted that Nero's name had a value of 666 in Hebrew. The title of the popes has this number value in Latin. This makes one believe that this number will reappear in various places all pointing to the deification of man, the dethroning of God, and the soul-destroying love of money.

Chapter Thirteen

The Jewel on the Dark Background

> *"All who dwell on the earth will worship him, whose names have not been written in the Book of Life of the Lamb slain from the foundation of the world." (Revelation 13:8 NKJV)*

It is here in this darkest of chapters that one of the greatest jewels of revelation is given: the Lamb of God was slain from the foundation of the world. At the dawn of time when God made His plan to create mankind in His image, He also made a plan to redeem the human race if they should fall into darkness. The Father, the Son and the Holy Spirit forged a plan, sealed by their everlasting faithful love and unbreakable word, that if necessary Jesus would be the sacrifice to heal the human race of the plague of sin. This verse also reveals that God foreknew who would believe in His Son and has had their names before Him written in the book of life from before our birth and before the world began. God is the great architect of the human race, and all of history is the outworking of a great plan. Does this deny the truth of human free will? No it defines that truth. No human being is the architect of their own salvation. All the glory goes to God. Human beings exercise their free will when they lay it down before Him in absolute surrender.

CHAPTER 14

THE BLESSEDNESS OF THE REDEEMED

The Blessedness of the Redeemed and the Calamity of Rejecting Christ

The Blessedness of those who will not bow the Knee to Antichrist

Revelation 14:1 I saw, and behold, the Lamb standing on Mount Zion, and with him a number, one hundred forty-four thousand, having his name, and the name of his Father, written on their foreheads. ² I heard a sound from heaven, like the sound of many waters, and like the sound of a great thunder. The sound which I heard was like that of harpists playing on their harps. ³ They sing a new song before the throne, and before the four living creatures and the elders. No one could learn the song except the one hundred forty-four thousand, those who had been redeemed out of the earth. ⁴ These are those who were not defiled with women, for they are virgins. These are those who follow the Lamb wherever he goes. These were redeemed by Jesus from among men, the first fruits to God and to the Lamb. ⁵ In their mouth was found no lie, for they are blameless.

John's gaze now turned from the dark figures of the Antichrist and the false prophet to the scene in heaven. He saw the redeemed standing on Mount Zion. This is not Zion in earthly Jerusalem, this is in heaven.

Chapter Fourteen

"But you have come to Mount Zion, and to the city of the living God, the heavenly Jerusalem, and to innumerable multitudes of angels, [23] to the general assembly and assembly of the firstborn who are enrolled in heaven, to God the Judge of all, to the spirits of just men made perfect, [24] to Jesus, the mediator of a new covenant, and to the blood of sprinkling that speaks better than that of Abel." (Hebrews 12:22-24)

The writer of Hebrews affirms the truth that believers on earth have already been joined together with a host of believers who have died and are alive around the throne of God in heaven. John is describing the unspeakable blessedness of those who have been redeemed and have not bowed the knee to the Antichrist and have not compromised with the world. John describes them as follows:

- Their number is 144,000 representing the perfect number of the redeemed throughout the gospel age. The number is perfect, and this indicates the unfolding of the perfect plan of God to redeem all who He has foreknown. These numbers all point to the meticulous plan that God has made and that is being worked out in the flow of human history.
- They have the Father's name in their foreheads. They have the Spirit of adoption and they belong to God the perfect Father.
- The voice of Jesus thunders like many waters among them. The joy and pride of Jesus is to present believers to His Father (Hebrews 2:12-13).
- They play harps, not literally, but their being is like an instrument producing constant music and song to God.
- They are singing a new song, the song of the redeemed that is exclusively theirs. Angels cannot sing it, nor even the four living creatures before the throne. Only those whose hearts have been cleansed by the blood of the Lamb may sing this song with full meaning.

- They are virgins undefiled by women. This does not cast aspersions on women since it refers to both men and women. It refers to spiritual virginity, keeping one's life pure and holy for God, and refusing to compromise with the pleasures of sin.
- The great mark of their lives is their simple obedience to Jesus the Lamb of God.
- They have no deceit in their mouths but have embraced truth and live in moral and spiritual transparency before men and God.

The Final Days of Gospel Proclamation

⁶I saw an angel flying in mid heaven, having an eternal Good News to proclaim to those who dwell on the earth, and to every nation, tribe, language, and people. ⁷He said with a loud voice, "Fear the Lord, and give him glory; for the hour of his judgment has come. Worship him who made the heaven, the earth, the sea, and the springs of waters!"

John saw another angel. This is a phrase that occurs several times in other places in Revelation (7:1; 8:3; 10:1 and 18:1). He saw 6 different angels in this chapter. The first one is sent to preach the gospel. It is not clear whether he is the invisible helper of evangelists or preaches himself. The great commission is given to the church, and it is normally the exclusive work of human beings to share the good news with others. Even in Acts 10 when Cornelius saw an angel, he was instructed to send for Peter to hear the gospel. Perhaps this verse indicates an extraordinary grace given to sinners as the curtain begins to fall on history.

The gospel that the angel preaches is not phrased in the typical words: "Repent of your sins and believe in Jesus Christ." While it may be assumed that this is the underlying message, the gospel that the angel preaches addresses four key challenges to every person:

Chapter Fourteen

1. "Fear God." The fear of the Lord is the beginning of wisdom (Proverbs 9:10). It is not the slavish dread of a cruel bully. It is the deep respect of the highest authority. People are to respect authority, first in their parents, then in society in obedience to the law, but ultimately as they fear God. Once the fear of God has been removed from a society all boundaries and restrictions will break down. People may escape the eyes of their parents and the police, but no one can escape the eyes of God.
2. "Give Glory to God." Most people boast of their achievements believing they have built up wealth and security by their hard work and intelligence. It is God alone who gives us power to get wealth (Deuteronomy 8:18). It is he who holds our breath and gives us life (Acts 17:25-28). The gospel challenges us to return in humility to God recognizing our total reliance on Him.
3. "Judgment has come." The history of the world demands a judgment day, and it is coming soon. We have the privilege of meeting Jesus as Saviour now, but if we refuse we will meet Him as judge.
4. "Worship God." All creatures will one day bow to God (Philippians 2:10-11) but it is our unique opportunity in the gospel age to bow voluntarily and surrender our lives entirely to Him.

Babylon is Fallen

[8] Another, a second angel, followed, saying, "Babylon the great has fallen, which has made all the nations to drink of the wine of the wrath of her sexual immorality."
[9] Another angel, a third, followed them, saying with a great voice, "If anyone worships the beast and his image, and receives a mark on his forehead, or on his hand, [10] he also will drink of the wine of the wrath of God, which is prepared unmixed in the cup of his anger. He will be tormented with fire and sulfur in the presence of the holy angels, and in the presence of the Lamb. [11] The smoke of their torment goes up forever and ever. They have no rest day and night, those who worship the beast

and his image, and whoever receives the mark of his name. [12] *Here is the patience of the saints, those who keep the commandments of God, and the faith of Jesus."*

A second angel announced the judgment of Babylon. This is the first mention of Babylon in Revelation and it is introduced with the assurance that she is fallen. The world's systems are doomed and their fate is already sealed, awaiting the outworking of God's inexorable plan. This great city is the capital of Antichrist's empire and has spread the evil of spiritual fornication throughout the earth. It was described as ripe for judgment. Though Babylon is described as a city, the scope of Babylon spreads like a spider's web through the whole of human civilisation world-wide. Babylon is the very spirit of the world in its fullest expression.

The third angel then announced the fearful judgment on those who followed the Antichrist and received his mark. Their punishment is described as follows:

- God's wrath will be in its full strength, without a trace of mercy. Most commonly judgment is poured out to humble the nations and bring them to repentance. But here God's wrath is poured out in full strength (literally "without mixture" or "undiluted") to punish evil doers.
- Their fate will be the eternal torment of hell. Hell is described as fire producing pain. Some have speculated that hell is where there is no presence of God. But here the Bible indicates that Jesus and the Holy Angels will themselves administer the righteous punishment for sins committed.
- There is no end indicated for this eternal punishment. They have no rest, no sleep in that dreadful state, and the smoke of the fires of hell rise forever and ever. This phrase "forever and ever" is applied to God in Revelation 10:1 and 15:7: *"God who lives for ever and ever."*

The Martyrs and the Final Revival

¹³ I heard the voice from heaven saying, "Write, 'Blessed are the dead who die in the Lord from now on.'"
"Yes," says the Spirit, "that they may rest from their labors; for their works follow with them."
¹⁴ I looked, and behold, a white cloud; and on the cloud one sitting like a son of man, having on his head a golden crown, and in his hand a sharp sickle. ¹⁵ Another angel came out of the temple, crying with a loud voice to him who sat on the cloud, "Send your sickle, and reap; for the hour to reap has come; for the harvest of the earth is ripe!" ¹⁶ He who sat on the cloud thrust his sickle on the earth, and the earth was reaped.

A voice from heaven commended the martyrs who died for their faith that they will find rest from their work and their labours will continue to bear fruit after their life on earth has ceased.

A fourth angel now came out of the temple in heaven speaking to Jesus that the time had come for Him to reap the earth. This is one of two distinct harvests, and this first one has no negative connotations. It is a revival through the direct activity of the Son of God. There are many verses like this in Revelation that give believers hope that as dark as the last days will be, there will be a huge world-wide revival at the end of time.

Judgment Poured Out

¹⁷ Another angel came out of the temple which is in heaven. He also had a sharp sickle. ¹⁸ Another angel came out from the altar, he who has power over fire, and he called with a great voice to him who had the sharp sickle, saying, "Send your sharp sickle, and gather the clusters of the vine of the earth, for the earth's grapes are fully ripe!" ¹⁹ The angel thrust his sickle into the earth, and gathered the vintage of the earth, and threw it into the great wine press of the wrath of God. ²⁰ The wine press was trodden outside of the city, and blood came out of the wine press, even to the bridles of the horses, as far as one thousand six hundred stadia.

The chapter ends with the fifth angel setting about reaping the earth in judgment. It is the day of God's wrath that is concluding the history of the planet earth. Sin has reached its full growth like grapes on a vine. Sinners, who could have turned to God and halted the progress of the poison of evil, refused to repent. Those who have ignored God's word will be carried on to the full expression of darkness and will be judged for it.

CHAPTER 15

THE 7 ANGELS AND THE 7 LAST PLAGUES

The Seven Angels Prepare to Pour out God's Wrath

Revelation 15 *[1] I saw another great and marvelous sign in the sky: seven angels having the seven last plagues, for in them God's wrath is finished. [2] I saw something like a sea of glass mixed with fire, and those who overcame the beast, his image, and the number of his name, standing on the sea of glass, having harps of God. [3] They sang the song of Moses, the servant of God, and the song of the Lamb, saying, "Great and marvelous are your works, Lord God, the Almighty!*
   Righteous and true are your ways, you King of the nations.
[4] Who wouldn't fear you, Lord, and glorify your name?
  For you only are holy.
  For all the nations will come and worship before you.
  For your righteous acts have been revealed."

John was now taken back to the moment of the opening of the seventh seal (Revelation 8:1) when the seven trumpets sounded and the judgments of God were poured out upon the earth. Verse one tells us that God's judgment is completed through these. God's ways are perfect and His judgments are perfectly appropriate to right every wrong. Perfect justice will prevail.

John saw again the scene in heaven, and it was the same view that he saw in chapter four. The difference is that there was now a host of saints who had overcome the Antichrist by not bowing the knee to him, indicating that many Christians will pass through tribulation. These believers have come through the fires of great persecution, whether through Nero or the last Antichrist. These saints sing the wonderful, exultant song of Moses and of the Lamb.

The song of Moses is in Exodus chapter 15 and it celebrated the liberation of the people of Israel from the hand of Pharaoh. The exodus was a type of the liberation of sinners from the power of Satan. Israel escaped when the lamb was slain at the first Passover. Sinners were set free from sin when Jesus the Lamb of God died at Passover and rose again three days later. So the first song of Moses was prophetic of the greater deliverance to come through the real Lamb of God on Calvary.

In the song of Moses and the Lamb, God is worshipped for His attributes. Here, it is God the King who is to be feared, for He is the perfect and righteous Judge. His works and His ways are glorified and it is to Him that all nations will finally come. He is the only true and living God. All must face Him in His holiness, and His righteous judgment of the world.

The angels receive the bowls of judgment

5 After these things I looked, and the temple of the tabernacle of the testimony in heaven was opened. 6 The seven angels who had the seven plagues came out, clothed with pure, bright linen, and wearing golden sashes around their breasts.
7 One of the four living creatures gave to the seven angels seven golden bowls full of the wrath of God, who lives forever and ever. 8 The temple was filled with smoke from the glory of God, and from his power. No one was able to enter into the temple, until the seven plagues of the seven angels would be finished.

Chapter Fifteen

John saw the enactment of a solemn ceremony. The seven angels stepped out of the temple of God in heaven. They resembled Jesus Christ, revealed in chapter 1, for they are clothed in pure bright linen and girded with a golden band around the chest. They stepped forward and one of the four living creatures committed into their hands the seven vials or bowls[32] each containing a judgment. The solemnity and gravity of this act was emphasised as the temple in heaven was filled with smoke and none was able to enter God's inner sanctuary. Was this because His face was bathed with tears and expressive of the deepest anguish that He must punish His beloved human race for their waywardness and lawless deeds? The sun was darkened at Calvary so that none might see the face of Jesus contorted with grief and sorrow as He bore the sin of the world. In the same way in the hour of judgment God drew a veil over His grief. God is a loving Father and every person straying far in sin is a lost son to Him.

---

[32] The Greek word is "phiale" meaning a broad, shallow bowl.

CHAPTER 16

THE 7 VIALS OF GOD'S WRATH

Revelation 16:1 *I heard a loud voice out of the temple, saying to the seven angels, "Go and pour out the seven bowls of the wrath of God on the earth!"*

The seven trumpets and the seven vial judgments describe the same events, but from different perspectives. It is not necessary to repeat the commentary given in chapter 8. In this section I will present a harmonisation of the two passages with an explanation of the apparent differences:

1st Trumpet and Vial.

² The first went, and poured out his bowl into the earth, and it became a harmful and evil sore on the people who had the mark of the beast, and who worshiped his image.

The first trumpet and first vial judgments both impact the earth. Revelation 8:7 describes the effect of this judgment on vegetation while Revelation 16:2 describes the impact on people.

2nd Trumpet and Vial.

³ The second angel poured out his bowl into the sea, and it became blood as of a dead man. Every living thing in the sea died.

The second trumpet and the second vial judgment both impact the sea by turning it into blood. There is a difference in the magnitude of these disasters. However it may be easily explained if the disaster had the immediate effect of killing one third of life in the sea, but after some time resulted in the death of all sea life

3rd Trumpet and Vial.

⁴ The third poured out his bowl into the rivers and springs of water, and they became blood. ⁵ I heard the angel of the waters saying, "You are righteous, who are and who were, you Holy One, because you have judged these things. ⁶ For they poured out the blood of the saints and the prophets, and you have given them blood to drink. They deserve this." ⁷ I heard the altar saying, "Yes, Lord God, the Almighty, true and righteous are your judgments."

The third trumpet and the third vial judgment both impact fresh water sources (fountains of waters and rivers). The multitudes that keep drinking of this contaminated water must be driven by desperate thirst given the awful bitter taste and the blood-like colour of the waters.

4th Trumpet and Vial

⁸ The fourth poured out his bowl on the sun, and it was given to him to scorch men with fire. ⁹ People were scorched with great heat, and people blasphemed the name of God who has the power over these plagues. They didn't repent and give him glory.

The fourth trumpet and the fourth vial both impact the sun. It is paradoxical that the sun is darkened and yet scorches people with great heat. Nevertheless it is not impossible that changes in the atmosphere would prevent light from penetrating a pall of pollution, while at the same time harmful rays of the sun such as ultra violet light may increase, causing sun burn and skin cancers. Revelation 8:12-13 mentions the sun, moon and stars, while chapter 16:8-9 focuses exclusively on the sun.

5th Trumpet and Vial

[10] The fifth poured out his bowl on the throne of the beast, and his kingdom was darkened. They gnawed their tongues because of the pain, [11] and they blasphemed the God of heaven because of their pains and their sores. They didn't repent of their works.

The fifth trumpet and the fifth vial both cause darkness on planet earth and severe torment but not death. Chapter 16:10-11 gives a brief summary while chapter 9:1-12 gives an extensive description of a swarm of demons released from the bottomless pit.

6th Trumpet and Vial

[12] The sixth poured out his bowl on the great river, the Euphrates. Its water was dried up, that the way might be prepared for the kings that come from the sunrise. [13] I saw coming out of the mouth of the dragon, and out of the mouth of the beast, and out of the mouth of the false prophet, three unclean spirits, something like frogs; [14] for they are spirits of demons, performing signs; which go out to the kings of the whole inhabited earth, to gather them together for the war of that great day of God, the Almighty.
[15] "Behold, I come like a thief. Blessed is he who watches, and keeps his clothes, so that he doesn't walk naked, and they see his shame." [16] He gathered them together into the place which is called in Hebrew, Megiddo.

When the sixth trumpet sounds, four angels are loosed from the Euphrates River which proceed to stir the nations into war. This action opens the way for the kings from the east and an enormous army to cross the dried up river presumably heading towards the Middle East. When the vial is poured out, 3 demons like frogs come out of the mouth of the Dragon sent out to deceive the nations and draw them into war. These are two separate but simultaneous events both involving first four and then three unseen evil spirits, bent on the same aim: the destruction of the human race through world war.

7th Trumpet and Vial

[17] The seventh poured out his bowl into the air. A loud voice came out of the temple of heaven, from the throne, saying, "It is done!" [18] There were lightnings, sounds, and thunders; and there was a great earthquake, such as was not since there were men on the earth, so great an earthquake, so mighty. [19] The great city was divided into three parts, and the cities of the nations fell. Babylon the great was remembered in the sight of God, to give to her the cup of the wine of the fierceness of his wrath. [20] Every island fled away, and the mountains were not found. [21] Great hailstones, about the weight of a talent, came down out of the sky on people. People blasphemed God because of the plague of the hail, for this plague is exceedingly severe.

When the seventh trumpet sounds and the seventh vial is poured out there are voices, lightning, thundering, an earthquake, and a great plague of hailstones. These things accompany the return of Christ and the end of the last Great War. The culmination of all things ends with an earthquake and the judgment of Babylon. Then begins the reign of Christ.

Harmonising the trumpet and vial judgments is not difficult and it is more credible than thinking of two Armageddons in the last days. It is not immediately obvious to grasp why these events were described in two separate accounts. Nevertheless it is not uncommon in the Bible.

Genesis chapter 1 describes the creation of mankind, followed by a more intimate view of the same act of creation in chapter 2. The four gospels frequently recount the same events, with apparent differences which are not difficult to harmonise.

The Message to the Heart

Revelation is a warning that as the return of Christ draws near, God will plead with the nations to repent by sending fearful judgments through natural disasters. These are all intended to turn sinners back to God and so escape the most fearful judgment of all: an eternity in hell.

CHAPTER 17

BABYLON

Babylon the Great

The book of Revelation is a presentation of opposites. Christ is revealed in chapter 1; the Antichrist is revealed in chapter 13. The church is revealed in chapters 2, 3, 12, 21 and 22. She is the bride clothed in pure linen and preparing herself for her bridegroom. The spirit of the world is revealed in chapters 17 and 18 as an unfaithful harlot. The bride is revealed as the Holy City of the heavenly Jerusalem. The world's systems are revealed as a corrupt and evil city called Babylon.

Babylon Revealed in the Old Testament

The Bible has much to say about Babylon. It appears in Genesis the book of origins and in the prophets where the darkness that inspires Babylon is revealed. In the history of God's people Babylon became the chief enemy of Judah in the 7th and 6th centuries BC. It was Babylon that destroyed Jerusalem and the temple, taking the nation into captivity.

Nimrod - The Founder of Babel/Babylon

"Cush begot Nimrod; he began to be a mighty one on the earth.

> He was a mighty hunter before the LORD; therefore it is said, "Like Nimrod the mighty hunter before the LORD." And the beginning of his kingdom was Babel, Erech, Accad, and Calneh, in the land of Shinar." (Genesis 10:8-10 NKJV)

The first mention of Babylon in the Bible is in Genesis 10:10. Nimrod, the grandson of Ham, was the founder of this city.[33] His name comes from a Hebrew word "marad" meaning "to rebel." The phrase *"before the LORD"* is misleading suggesting he was a believer. This is the same Hebrew word used in Genesis 6:11 *"The whole earth was corrupt before God."* It indicates that Nimrod's rebellious activities were under God's scrutiny, not that they were done in faith. Nimrod was a rebel and there is a legend that he even shot an arrow into heaven at God.[34] Rabbis believed Nimrod himself built the tower of Babel and they frequently called it "The House of Nimrod."[35]

The Tower Of Babel/Babylon

> "Indeed the people are one and they all have one language, and this is what they begin to do; now nothing that they propose to do will be withheld from them. Come, let Us go down and there confuse their language, that they may not understand one another's speech." So the LORD scattered them abroad from there over the face of all the earth, and they ceased building the city. Therefore its name is called Babel, because there the LORD confused the language of all the earth; and from there the LORD scattered them abroad over the face of all the earth." (Genesis 11:6-9 NKJV)

---

[33] Most English translations have two different transliterations of one Hebrew word "Babel" and "Babylon." This is misleading for there is only one word in Hebrew.

[34] For this and other legends about Nimrod see the entry in *The Jewish Encyclopedia,* 1906. The article affirms the Rabbinical view that Nimrod was an archetypal rebel.

[35] Ibid.

Chapter Seventeen

The tower of Babel/Babylon in Genesis 11 was a monument to the ambition and arrogance of man. The unification of all nations in one language is still the goal of the Antichrist system as then there will be no limit to what can be achieved. God divided the nations through languages at Babel to slow down the progress of sin.

Globalisation and the spread of communication through the internet and other electronic means are slowly but surely allowing the whole world to operate as one. The word Babylon means confusion, which was caused by God to slow down the development of an anti-God unity in the human race.

The Spirit Behind Babylon

> *"How you are fallen from heaven, O Lucifer, son of the morning! How you are cut down to the ground, you who weakened the nations! For you have said in your heart: 'I will ascend into heaven, I will exalt my throne above the stars of God; I will also sit on the mount of the congregation On the farthest sides of the north; I will ascend above the heights of the clouds, I will be like the Most High.' (Isaiah 14:12-14 NKJV)*

Isaiah chapters 13 and 14 are the beginning of a series of prophecies against the nations around Israel. When Isaiah gave this prophecy Babylon was not the dominant world power and would not be for another hundred years. Yet Isaiah began his prophecies about the nations with Babylon. This is because the Bible identifies this city as the head and fountain of all nations.

In chapter 14 Isaiah spoke to the spirit behind the king of Babylon and addressed Satan himself. Babylon had embraced the same arrogance as Lucifer the prince of darkness and he is the inspiration and power behind it and all world empires.

Babylon - The Head of Gold

In Daniel chapter 2, Nebuchadnezzar had a dream and saw a statue:
> " As for this image, its head was of fine gold, its breast and its arms of silver, its belly and its thighs of brass, [33] its legs of iron, its feet part of iron, and part of clay." (Daniel 2:32-33)

This was a vision of the spirit of the world changing its form like a chameleon through each successive generation. It also represents the weakness of the world's rulers and their governments. The Head of Gold is not only the head in order of historical sequence. Babylon is the source and fountain of spiritual power behind all nations. The power behind Babylon is Lucifer, and this is the unchanging truth behind world empires. All human power presents a head of gold, to dazzle and impress, but stands on feet of clay which are weak and certain to collapse. This is also true of all world religions and even Christian religious institutions if they build for the glory of man not God. Only the church that is built by Jesus Christ will stand for eternity.

Babylon - The Persecutor of the Saints

Daniel and other believers were fiercely threatened and persecuted in Babylon, indicating that believers will have to contend for their faith as they live and work in the world. In Revelation 18:4 God commanded his people to come out of Babylon. Some have interpreted this to mean that believers should live in remote places or monasteries to keep themselves pure. But Daniel demonstrated that it is possible to be in Babylon geographically but not in Babylon spiritually. Daniel never allowed the spirit of Babylon to corrupt his faith even though he rose to the highest office in the government. In order to preserve his faith and keep his heart pure Daniel had to be willing to die, preferring to be killed by lions rather than stop praying. God demonstrated that He was able to keep His people through the fiercest trials if they will trust and obey Him.

Chapter Seventeen

Babylon and Rome

"She who is in Babylon, chosen together with you, greets you"
(1 Peter 5:13).

Peter wrote these words while he was in Rome. He referred to Rome as Babylon, indicating that the name Babylon is not to identify just one world power but all centres of human government, both political and financial. Peter also spoke of the believers in Rome personifying them as a woman (she who is in Babylon).

Babylon - The Great Harlot

***Revelation 17:1** One of the seven angels who had the seven bowls came and spoke with me, saying, "Come here. I will show you the judgment of the great prostitute who sits on many waters, [2] with whom the kings of the earth committed sexual immorality, and those who dwell in the earth were made drunken with the wine of her sexual immorality." [3] He carried me away in the Spirit into a wilderness. I saw a woman sitting on a scarlet-colored animal, full of blasphemous names, having seven heads and ten horns. [4] The woman was dressed in purple and scarlet, and decked with gold and precious stones and pearls, having in her hand a golden cup full of abominations and the impurities of the sexual immorality of the earth. [5] And on her forehead a name was written, "MYSTERY, BABYLON THE GREAT, THE MOTHER OF THE PROSTITUTES AND OF THE ABOMINATIONS OF THE EARTH." [6] I saw the woman drunken with the blood of the saints, and with the blood of the martyrs of Jesus. When I saw her, I wondered with great amazement.*

Babylon is the great whore, the opposite of the Bride. The whore is unfaithful to God, and this speaks of the spiritual apostasy of many nations, which will allow the Antichrist to take power and rule. Babylon is the supreme chameleon holding no moral or spiritual values. The only principles governing behaviour in Babylon are self-enrichment and pleasure.

The rulers of earth have committed spiritual fornication, and so have the multitudes of citizens who have willingly followed their lead. John saw the inhabitants of the earth as satiated with the drunken pleasures that abound in hearts and lives that are unfaithful to God.

John saw the woman in a wilderness, which is an accurate description of the state of the world without God. John saw the unity and harmony between the beast and Babylon. The beast is the Antichrist of chapter 13.

The woman was decked in luxurious clothing and covered with gold and gems of fabulous wealth, but she was not drinking of the cup of Christ. The magnificent wealth of the mother of harlots speaks of the riches of the popes, the royal houses of Europe and the vast financial empires of modern business. The great whore was drinking of morally degrading abominations and of the unclean activities of those who are unfaithful to God. The word "fornication" is repeated often in this chapter and indicates that God is like a rejected suitor. He has done all He can to bring sinners to repentance and win their love. But sinners have spurned His approaches and turned their back on Him, worshipping false gods and indulging in repugnant pleasures.

John saw her name: *"MYSTERY, BABYLON THE GREAT, THE MOTHER OF HARLOTS AND OF THE ABOMINATIONS OF THE EARTH."* The Bible speaks of the mystery of iniquity indicating that the power of evil defies logical definition and explanation. There is an element of madness and insanity in the practice of evil.

Then John saw that the woman was also drunk with the blood of the saints, and that there were a large number of martyrs at the hands of this world system.

The Angel Explains All

[7] The angel said to me, "Why do you wonder? I will tell you the mystery

Chapter Seventeen

of the woman, and of the beast that carries her, which has the seven heads and the ten horns.

An angel approached John and proceeded to explain to him the repulsive vision before him:

The Beast

⁸ The beast that you saw was, and is not; and is about to come up out of the abyss and to go into destruction. Those who dwell on the earth and whose names have not been written in the book of life from the foundation of the world will marvel when they see that the beast was, and is not, and shall be present. ⁹ Here is the mind that has wisdom. The seven heads are seven mountains, on which the woman sits. ¹⁰ They are seven kings. Five have fallen, the one is, the other has not yet come. When he comes, he must continue a little while. ¹¹ The beast that was, and is not, is himself also an eighth, and is of the seven; and he goes to destruction.

The angel used enigmatic words to describe the identity of the Antichrist, the beast. The Antichrist ascends out of the bottomless pit, indicating his demonically inspired nature. His destination is certain and already known: perdition, literally "the place of destruction."

The seven heads of Antichrist are seven mountains, which symbolise nations. John is also told that there are a total of seven kings. It is not clear whether this refers to individual rulers or kingdoms as a whole. The angel says that one of the kings "is, which seems to be referring to the Roman Empire. What were then the five empires which had fallen prior to the Roman Empire? World History would indicate the following:

1. Egypt – fallen.
2. Assyria – fallen.
3. Babylon – fallen.

4. Persia – fallen.
5. Greece – fallen.
6. Rome – The one that is.
7. The one who is not yet come, who will continue for a short time. (Could this refer to Hitler?).
8. The final Antichrist who is of the 7.

This may be the meaning of this enigmatic phraseology.

The Ten Horns and the Waters

[12]{.sup} The ten horns that you saw are ten kings who have received no kingdom as yet, but they receive authority as kings, with the beast, for one hour. [13]{.sup} These have one mind, and they give their power and authority to the beast. [14]{.sup} These will war against the Lamb, and the Lamb will overcome them, for he is Lord of lords, and King of kings, and those who are with him are called, chosen, and faithful." [15]{.sup} He said to me, "The waters which you saw, where the prostitute sits, are peoples, multitudes, nations, and languages. [16]{.sup} The ten horns which you saw, and the beast, these will hate the prostitute, and will make her desolate, and will make her naked, and will eat her flesh, and will burn her utterly with fire. [17]{.sup} For God has put in their hearts to do what he has in mind, and to be of one mind, and to give their kingdom to the beast, until the words of God should be accomplished. [18]{.sup} The woman whom you saw is the great city, which reigns over the kings of the earth."

The ten horns are a confederation of nations who become powerful on the coat tails of the Antichrist. They are united in their ardent support for this evil ruler. Their battle is with Jesus Christ the Lamb of God, and though His Coming may tarry, when He returns the war will be settled in the briefest period, since He is the unconquerable King of Kings and Lord of Lords.

Revelation 17:16 indicates that there will be internal disorder in the Antichrist system and that this disorder will be the final downfall of

Babylon. God will put it into the hearts of this confederacy of nations to hate the centres of wealth and power, and destroy Babylon.

Finally the angel identified the woman Babylon as the great capital city of the Antichrist. This could be one city, but there will always be more than one such city in every age. Rome, London, New York, Moscow, Shanghai, Hong Kong and Berlin are all candidates in history. Such cities have beautiful buildings and monuments, but all have a dark side as centres of evil. Financial centres such as Wall St attract people gluttonous for wealth. The US government disposes of billions of dollars each year and this vast river of money inevitably attracts corruption and avarice on a huge scale.

The European Union

In Daniel chapter 2 Nebuchadnezzar saw a statue with Babylon as the Head of Gold, and the legs representing the Roman Empire. Daniel interpreted this vision as a prophecy of the history of the world till the return of Christ. Daniel saw that the Roman Empire (the legs of the statue) would continue in different forms from the pagan Roman Empire. The Roman Empire fell in the middle of the 5th century AD. This was soon replaced by the Roman Catholic Church and the power of the popes who ruled with religious and political power throughout the Middle Ages. The Holy Roman Empire was a confederacy of nations dominated by Germany that was a union of the papacy with political power. Charlemagne was the first to be crowned as emperor by the popes on 25th December AD 800. When Hitler came to power, he announced the arrival of the 3rd Reich, which was a 3rd revival of the Holy Roman Empire of Charlemagne. (The 2nd Reich of 1870 was the second revival of Charlemagne's empire and was declared by Kaiser/Emperor Wilhelm I. The 2nd Reich ended in 1918 with the fall of Kaiser Wilhelm II). Hitler's 3rd Reich modelled itself on ancient Rome. His followers designed standards in the Roman style while Hitler planned to remodel Berlin to outstrip the glory of ancient Rome.

After the Second World War ended in 1945 the Treaty of Rome of 1957 signalled the beginning of the European Union which continues to this day. Many see in this confederation of nations the continuation of the Roman Empire, represented by the toes of the statue seen by Nebuchadnezzar.

The European Parliament building was recently designed and constructed using a painting completed in 1563 of the Tower of Babel by Pieter Brueghel. During construction of the new parliament building, a poster was issued by the EU, showing the tower of Babel and carrying the slogan: "Many tongues, one voice." A crane in the background was shown indicating they were rebuilding the ancient tower of Babel. In 1984 the elections to the European Parliament were marked in Britain by a set of stamps with two designs. One shows a woman riding a beast or bull led by a winged boy. The animal was riding over seven hills, or waves of the sea. This was to represent the pagan goddess Europa, whom Jupiter led away in the form of a bull.

The new Brussels headquarters of the Council of Europe also has a bronze statue of a woman riding a beast, and the beast is depicted riding on waves, just as in Revelation 17. In the history of Israel there were two captivities, each of a very different nature. The Egyptian captivity was one of abject slavery, while the Babylonian one was one of assimilation and compromise. In Egypt, the people of God were hated and kept in isolation. In Babylon, they were given opportunities and encouraged to buy land and houses and settle down. There are two kinds of attack on Christians today - the first through direct persecution, the second by seducing believers to worldliness and compromise. The European Union has never directly persecuted Christians but the prevailing atmosphere in Europe is one of stifling seduction.

So is the European Union Babylon? The spirit of Babylon is not confined to Europe but is prevalent throughout the whole world.

Chapter Seventeen

Is it the revived Roman Empire which is the current main manifestation of the spirit of Babylon? It is premature to identify the EU as the centre of evil described in Revelation 17 and 18. It is nevertheless astonishing that EU politicians should have the boldness to associate themselves with the scheme of human pride recounted in the construction of the tower of Babel and thereby with the evil world system described in Revelation 17 and 18.

Will the Antichrist arise from among its member states? Currently the European Union is distinctly humanist not Christian in its philosophy. The "Ode to Joy" is the anthem of the EU and is a poem by Friedrich Schiller set to music by Beethoven and celebrating humanity. Despite this non-Christian philosophy the EU has certainly not yet demonstrated the evil tendencies of Antichrist governments such as those of Nero, Hitler, Stalin, or Mao. If Antichrist is to arise in Europe then there are major political and economic upheavals that will have to take place before there is a universal cry for a dictator.

CHAPTER 18

THE FALL OF BABYLON

The Fall Is Announced

Revelation 18:1 *After these things, I saw another angel coming down out of the sky, having great authority. The earth was illuminated with his glory.* [2] *He cried with a mighty voice, saying, "Fallen, fallen is Babylon the great, and she has become a habitation of demons, a prison of every unclean spirit, and a prison of every unclean and hateful bird!* [3] *For all the nations have drunk of the wine of the wrath of her sexual immorality, the kings of the earth committed sexual immorality with her, and the merchants of the earth grew rich from the abundance of her luxury."*

[4] *I heard another voice from heaven, saying, "Come out of her, my people, that you have no participation in her sins, and that you don't receive of her plagues,* [5] *for her sins have reached to the sky, and God has remembered her iniquities.* [6] *Return to her just as she returned, and repay her double as she did, and according to her works. In the cup which she mixed, mix to her double.* [7] *However much she glorified herself, and grew wanton, so much give her of torment and mourning. For she says in her heart, 'I sit a queen, and am no widow, and will in no way see mourning.'* [8] *Therefore in one day her plagues will come: death, mourning, and famine; and she will be utterly burned with fire; for the*

Chapter Eighteen

Lord God who has judged her is strong.

John then saw a mighty angel having great authority announcing with a great cry the fall of Babylon. The angel echoed the cries of Isaiah and Jeremiah, for this was not the first time Babylon had fallen:

> "Babylon is fallen, is fallen! And all the carved images of her gods He has broken to the ground." (Isaiah 21:9 NKJV)
> "Babylon is suddenly fallen and destroyed: wail for her." (Jeremiah 51:8)
> "It shall be, when you have finished reading this book, that you shall bind a stone to it, and cast it into the middle of the Euphrates: [64] and you shall say, Thus shall Babylon sink, and shall not rise again because of the evil that I will bring on her; and they shall be weary. Thus far are the words of Jeremiah.." (Jeremiah 51:63-64)

Her fall did not make her a habitation of every unclean spirit, but rather this was the cause of her fall. Her sins were her spiritual fornication and her love of luxury, sins which are characteristics of society in the 21st century.

The angel cried to the people of God to come out of Babylon, to utterly forsake the love of luxury, the worship of money, the compromise with immoral standards of behavior and false religions. Daniel is a perfect example of a believer who came out of Babylon but did not leave it geographically. We must get Babylon out of our system by radical repentance and intentional discipleship, denying ourselves and taking up our cross.

The exhortation was coupled with a warning that believers who do not forsake the spirit of the world will partake of Babylon's judgment. The angel lamented that the sins of Babylon had reached to heaven, to the ears of God. Now God was about to reward her double for her iniquity. These will be the days of a great reversal. Those who once enjoyed luxury will now suffer deprivation and punishment. Those who forsook the world will now be rewarded in heaven.

Babylon was rebuked by the angel for her pride and sense of invincibility. Wealth always produces a false sense of security, for it is only righteousness that will protect any person from the greatest disaster of all which is to stand with guilt and shame before God on the Day of Judgment.

The angel then prophesied the sudden and total collapse of Babylon in the space of one single day. The Bible shows that the empires of men, with their palaces and monuments, are only sandcastles which will all be swept away by the next wave of the sea. So many physical and ideological edifices look strong and impregnable, but they will collapse. Communism, capitalism, false religions and philosophies all look intimidating, but they are all built on sand and will all finally crumble, fall and be no more.

The World Mourns the Fall of Babylon

[9] The kings of the earth, who committed sexual immorality and lived wantonly with her, will weep and wail over her, when they look at the smoke of her burning, [10] standing far away for the fear of her torment, saying, 'Woe, woe, the great city, Babylon, the strong city! For your judgment has come in one hour.' [11] The merchants of the earth weep and mourn over her, for no one buys their merchandise any more; [12] merchandise of gold, silver, precious stones, pearls, fine linen, purple, silk, scarlet, all expensive wood, every vessel of ivory, every vessel made of most precious wood, and of brass, and iron, and marble; [13] and cinnamon, incense, perfume, frankincense, wine, olive oil, fine flour, wheat, sheep, horses, chariots, and people's bodies and souls. [14] The fruits which your soul lusted after have been lost to you, and all things that were dainty and sumptuous have perished from you, and you will find them no more at all. [15] The merchants of these things, who were made rich by her, will stand far away for the fear of her torment,

weeping and mourning; [16] *saying, 'Woe, woe, the great city, she who was dressed in fine linen, purple, and scarlet, and decked with gold and precious stones and pearls!* [17] *For in an hour such great riches are made desolate.' Every ship master, and everyone who sails anywhere, and mariners, and as many as gain their living by sea, stood far away,* [18] *and cried out as they looked at the smoke of her burning, saying, 'What is like the great city?'* [19] *They cast dust on their heads, and cried, weeping and mourning, saying, 'Woe, woe, the great city, in which all who had their ships in the sea were made rich by reason of her great wealth!' For she is made desolate in one hour.*

The fall of Babylon will be greeted with fearful dismay by many kings of earth who feasted on her wealth, and by the merchants who made themselves rich by trading with her. The kings of earth referred to here will not be part of the confederacy of nations that are in direct partnership with the Antichrist, for in the previous chapter it is recorded that the nations of the confederacy are the ones who bring about her destruction.

These wailing kings and merchants will observe the destruction from a distance and witness the smoke of her burning. The city will fall in one hour, and it is conceivable that Babylon will be destroyed by a nuclear holocaust. The Bible indicates that the last days will be a time of peace, but that it will be false peace followed by sudden destruction.

> *" "As the days of Noah were, so will be the coming of the Son of Man. For as in those days which were before the flood they were eating and drinking, marrying and giving in marriage, until the day that Noah entered into the ship, and they didn't know until the flood came, and took them all away, so will be the coming of the Son of Man." (Matthew 24:37-39)*
>
> *"For when they are saying, "Peace and safety," then sudden destruction will come on them, like birth pains on a pregnant woman; and they will in no way escape." (1 Thessalonians 5:3)*

The day will come when Babylon will be destroyed by the armies of the Antichrist's confederacy probably in a sudden pre-emptive military strike.

The Finality of the Fall of Babylon

[20] *"Rejoice over her, O heaven, you saints, apostles, and prophets; for God has judged your judgment on her."* [21] *A mighty angel took up a stone like a great millstone and cast it into the sea, saying, "Thus with violence will Babylon, the great city, be thrown down, and will be found no more at all.* [22] *The voice of harpists, minstrels, flute players, and trumpeters will be heard no more at all in you. No craftsman, of whatever craft, will be found any more at all in you. The sound of a mill will be heard no more at all in you.* [23] *The light of a lamp will shine no more at all in you. The voice of the bridegroom and of the bride will be heard no more at all in you; for your merchants were the princes of the earth; for with your sorcery all the nations were deceived.* [24] *In her was found the blood of prophets and of saints, and of all who have been slain on the earth."*

The nations will grieve at her passing, but heaven will rejoice for the days of vengeance. God commands His people to love their enemies:

> "But I tell you, love your enemies, bless those who curse you, do good to those who hate you, and pray for those who mistreat you and persecute you." (Matthew 5:44)

But God does not intend that violent people should escape due punishment if they will not repent. God's people long for grace and mercy to prevail, but they also long for justice.

> "Don't seek revenge yourselves, beloved, but give place to God's wrath. For it is written, "Vengeance belongs to me; I will repay, says the Lord." (Romans 12:19)

Chapter Eighteen

The judgment of Babylon will be final and irreversible. The playing of music and singing of songs will be gone forever. No longer will they give and be given in marriage and her destruction will be terrible and complete.

CHAPTER 19

THE COMING OF CHRIST

Heaven's Joy at the Fall of Babylon

Revelation 19:1 *After these things I heard something like a loud voice of a great multitude in heaven, saying, "Hallelujah! Salvation, power, and glory belong to our God: ² for true and righteous are his judgments. For he has judged the great prostitute, who corrupted the earth with her sexual immorality, and he has avenged the blood of his servants at her hand."*
³ A second said, "Hallelujah! Her smoke goes up forever and ever." ⁴ The twenty-four elders and the four living creatures fell down and worshiped God who sits on the throne, saying, "Amen! Hallelujah!"
⁵ A voice came from the throne, saying, "Give praise to our God, all you his servants, you who fear him, the small and the great!"

These first five verses of chapter 19 conclude the portrayal of Babylon and her fall with a description of the response of heaven. There was no mention of joy at the downfall of the world's systems, but there was a note of solemn praise that justice had prevailed. Babylon shed the blood of righteous men and women, and now the day of the Lord will dawn. Divine judgment will be meted out with perfect justice. History cries out for this, that every wrong be righted, and that great process will begin with the return of Christ.

Chapter Nineteen

The Marriage Supper of the Lamb

⁶ *I heard something like the voice of a great multitude, and like the voice of many waters, and like the voice of mighty thunders, saying, "Hallelujah! For the Lord our God, the Almighty, reigns!* ⁷ *Let us rejoice and be exceedingly glad, and let us give the glory to him. For the marriage of the Lamb has come, and his wife has made herself ready."* ⁸ *It was given to her that she would array herself in bright, pure, fine linen: for the fine linen is the righteous acts of the saints.*
⁹ *He said to me, "Write, 'Blessed are those who are invited to the marriage supper of the Lamb.'" He said to me, "These are true words of God."*
¹⁰ *I fell down before his feet to worship him. He said to me, "Look! Don't do it! I am a fellow bondservant with you and with your brothers who hold the testimony of Jesus. Worship God, for the testimony of Jesus is the Spirit of Prophecy."*

The multitudes of heaven will praise God and their voice will resound like thunder. Now the praises for the righteous acts of vengeance turn to praises of boundless joy because the marriage supper of the Lamb is about to begin. Weddings are times of pure joy, when a couple celebrates their love for one another. The day will have been prepared over many months and special clothes are worn and the best food is presented. The multitudes of believers are the bride and they are clothed in the pure fine linen of righteous acts. It will be a day of unlimited joy as believers see the fulfillment of their faith in everlasting union with God.

The person who spoke with John was so glorious in appearance that John fell at his feet to worship him. But John was stopped from doing so, with the astonishing words that this is none other than an ordinary believer, now glorified in heaven. Eternal life is so much more than existence without end; the Bible reveals it is life on another plane through union with God. We partake of the divine nature, and of the pulsating brightness and bliss that fills God's own being. It is obvious that believers will never be equal to God, but the plan of God is to share His own life with His followers, to make them partakers of His substance even as Eve was bone of Adam's bone and flesh of his flesh. We are to have His love, His holiness, His joy, His peace and His life flowing through our spiritual veins.

> "Grace to you and peace be multiplied in the knowledge of God and of Jesus our Lord, *3 seeing* that his divine power has granted to us all things that pertain to life and godliness, through the knowledge of him who called us by his own glory and virtue; *4 by* which he has granted to us his precious and exceedingly great promises; that through these you may become partakers of the divine nature." (2 Peter 1:2-4)

> "Whom he predestined, those he also called. Whom he called, those he also justified. Whom he justified, those he also glorified." (Romans 8:30)

The Second Coming of Christ

11 I saw the heaven opened, and behold, a white horse, and he who sat on it is called Faithful and True. In righteousness he judges and makes war. 12 His eyes are a flame of fire, and on his head are many crowns. He has names written and a name written which no one knows but he himself. 13 He is clothed in a garment sprinkled with blood. His name is called "The Word of God." 14 The armies which are in heaven followed him on white horses, clothed in white, pure, fine linen. 15 Out of his mouth proceeds a sharp, double-edged sword, that with it he should strike the nations. He will rule them with an iron rod. He treads the wine press of the fierceness of the wrath of God, the Almighty. 16 He has on his garment and on his thigh a name written, "KING OF KINGS, AND LORD OF LORDS."

Chapter Nineteen

John now saw heaven open and Jesus rode forth on a white horse. This is a detailed description of the events accompanying the last trumpet. It is at this moment that the dead in Christ shall rise and that believers will meet with the Lord in the air. John was told three titles of Jesus Christ:

- "Faithful and True," describing the unchangeable character of His promises and His personality. He cannot break His own word and the great source of believers' joy is His faithfulness that will never fail and never disappoint whoever trusts in Him.
- "The Word of God," describing Jesus as the expression of God's person, God's love and God's righteousness.
- "King of Kings and Lord of Lords," describing His absolute authority over all humanity. All must bow to Him either freely or reluctantly.

John also saw the following details:

- His eyes were like a flame of fire, piercing, fearful and searching the hearts.
- His clothing had been dipped in blood. He appeared as if He were fresh from His victory at Calvary where He shed His blood.
- Out of His mouth went the sharp sword that would strike the nations. Jesus Christ will fight the final battle by speaking the word of power that shall slay His enemies.
  "And then the lawless one will be revealed, whom the Lord will consume with the breath of His mouth and destroy with the brightness of His coming." (2 Thessalonians 2:8)
- Christ treads the winepress of God's wrath. The day of anger and of vengeance has come.

John also saw the host of believers coming with Him clothed in white linen and riding on white horses. To follow in the train of Jesus is to side with righteousness, love and victory. In this life it is believers who are persecuted and down-trodden in many parts of the world. In the day of His return there will be great reversal and those who suffered loss will share with Christ in His triumph over evil.

The Final Battle between Christ and Antichrist

[17] I saw an angel standing in the sun. He cried with a loud voice, saying to all the birds that fly in the sky, "Come! Be gathered together to the great supper of God, [18] that you may eat the flesh of kings, the flesh of captains, the flesh of mighty men, and the flesh of horses and of those who sit on them, and the flesh of all men, both free and slave, and small and great." [19] I saw the beast, and the kings of the earth, and their armies, gathered together to make war against him who sat on the horse, and against his army. [20] The beast was taken, and with him the false prophet who worked the signs in his sight, with which he deceived those who had received the mark of the beast and those who worshiped his image. These two were thrown alive into the lake of fire that burns with sulfur. [21] The rest were killed with the sword of him who sat on the horse, the sword which came out of his mouth. All the birds were filled with their flesh.

It is hard to believe that Antichrist, the final dictator, will presume to fight with Christ Himself in all His unveiled glory and accompanied with the armies of heaven. Yet this is what John now saw. The prelude to the final battle was the appearance of an angel standing in the sun and calling to the birds of the air to come and feast on the bodies of the slain. The battle is not described and it may be presumed that it will not last more than a few minutes. Christ will speak with wrath and thunder and His enemies will fall down slain before Him.

The Antichrist and the false prophet were captured, not killed. They were not reserved for Judgment Day but were immediately cast alive into hell: the lake of fire. The end of this age will be swift and sudden. The final days will be in the throes of world war, leading up to Armageddon in the Middle East. At this time also Babylon will fall by a sudden attack of the Antichrist's confederacy. Then will come the last trumpet and the events described in this chapter. It may be assumed that Christ will do battle and overcome His enemies quickly. Christ shall then stand triumphant on the earth surrounded by His beloved people.

CHAPTER 20

THE MILENNIUM AND THE LAST JUDGMENT

The Millennium[36]

Revelation 20:1 *I saw an angel coming down out of heaven, having the key of the abyss and a great chain in his hand. ² He seized the dragon, the old serpent, which is the devil and Satan, who deceives the whole inhabited earth, and bound him for a thousand years, ³ and cast him into the abyss, and shut it, and sealed it over him, that he should deceive the nations no more, until the thousand years were finished. After this, he must be freed for a short time. ⁴ I saw thrones, and they sat on them, and judgment was given to them. I saw the souls of those who had been beheaded for the testimony of Jesus, and for the word of God, and such as didn't worship the beast nor his image, and didn't receive the mark on their forehead and on their hand. They lived and reigned with Christ for a thousand years. ⁵ The rest of the dead didn't live until the thousand years were finished. This is the first resurrection. ⁶ Blessed and holy is he*

---

[36] The view presented here is known as the Pre-millennial interpretation. There are two further interpretations of the millennium: 1. Amillennialism, which is the belief that it is to be interpreted symbolically not literally and refers to the present gospel age. 2. Post-millennialism, the belief that the millennium will be ushered in by the spread of the gospel leading to a thousand years of peace preceding the return of Christ.

who has part in the first resurrection. Over these, the second death has no power, but they will be priests of God and of Christ, and will reign with him one thousand years.

Immediately after the return of Christ, John saw an angel descending from heaven and binding the Devil in the bottomless pit. This bottomless pit was mentioned in chapter 9 when floods of demons were released at the sound of the fifth trumpet. Now they are all imprisoned again without exception. Their captivity will last one thousand years.

During this period Christ will rule the earth with His faithful followers. It might seem at first sight that it is only a small group of believers who will reign with Christ, namely those who had been beheaded for their witness to Jesus, and had not bowed the knee to the Antichrist. However from other scriptures it is clear that that all believers will rise from the dead at the return of Christ, not just those who have been martyred:

> "For the Lord himself will descend from heaven with a shout, with the voice of the archangel, and with God's trumpet. The dead in Christ will rise first, [17] then we who are alive, who are left, will be caught up together with them in the clouds, to meet the Lord in the air. So we will be with the Lord forever." (1 Thessalonians 4:16-17)

The simplest interpretation of the millennium is that there will be a literal reign of one thousand years on the earth by Jesus when He returns. There are many prophecies of the millennium in the Old Testament. Zechariah 14 teaches that when Christ returns He will come with all the saints.

> "And in that day His feet will stand on the Mount of Olives, which faces Jerusalem on the east. And the Mount of Olives shall be split in two, from east to west, making a very large valley;

> *half of the mountain shall move toward the north and half of it toward the south.... Thus the LORD my God will come, and all the saints with You.... And in that day it shall be that living waters shall flow from Jerusalem, half of them toward the eastern sea and half of them toward the western sea; In both summer and winter it shall occur. And the LORD shall be King over all the earth. In that day it shall be-- "The LORD is one," And His name one." (Zechariah 14:4-9 NKJV)*

This passage gives further details about when the millennium will begin. Jesus will stand upon the Mount of Olives. The Mount will then split in two and water will flow out eastwards to the Dead Sea and westwards to the Mediterranean. The salt laden seas will then be healed. This prophecy is repeated in Ezekiel 47 and Joel 3:18. The Lion will lie down with the lamb (See Isaiah 65:20, 11:6-9, Psalm 72:8-14) and there will be a thousand year period of the benign rule of Christ.

Why will God inaugurate the Millennium? There is no explicit reason given in scripture. It may be that through the Millennium God will prove to mankind that the devil is not the cause of evil in the human race. The cause of evil is the wrong exercise of personal moral choice. If the devil had not existed, man would still have to prove himself by choosing the tree of life rather than the tree of the knowledge of good and evil. Revelation 20 indicates that at the end of the Millennium, the devil will be released from the bottomless pit and will once more deceive the nations. This is of course only possible to those who are unconverted. The point is that even during the benign rule of Christ not everyone will accept His Lordship in their lives. Christ will certainly not rule through dictatorship, but rather through the power of His love. Mankind is free to choose or reject Christ. Every human being is what he or she is by deliberate choice not by force of circumstances.

It must be assumed that many unbelievers will survive the violent convulsions that precede the return of Christ and will then live on into the millennial reign. This will then form the group of nations who will be deceived by Satan at the end of the millennium.

We may ask how believers with a new resurrection body will live alongside sinners who are still with a mortal body. There is a precedent for this because Christ appeared to the disciples with a resurrection body and interacted with them and even ate with them.

It may be asked how Christ will rule? No doubt He will continue to rule His people by the agency of the indwelling Spirit and His people will then administer His benign and loving rule. We may wonder why all unbelievers will not be converted after the visible return of Christ? The answer is that Jesus stood before Pilate and Caiaphas and yet these two men were not the least softened by the experience. Though some will harden their hearts, it is to be hoped that many sinners will turn in full surrender to Jesus.

The questions are innumerable and since the Bible does not give us enough information we can only speculate. Fortunately the Bible does not make our understanding of the Millennium a key foundation or condition of salvation!

Satan's Last Gasp

[7] And after the thousand years, Satan will be released from his prison, [8] and he will come out to deceive the nations which are in the four corners of the earth, Gog and Magog, to gather them together to the war; the number of whom is as the sand of the sea. [9] They went up over the width of the earth, and surrounded the camp of the saints, and the beloved city. Fire came down out of heaven from God, and devoured them. [10] The devil who deceived them was thrown into the lake of fire and sulfur, where the beast and the false prophet are also. They will be tormented day and night forever and ever.

The thousand years will end when Satan is released and is allowed to deceive the nations once more. He will stir up the nations referred to as

Gog and Magog, which may be taken to indicate the nations that spearhead the rejection of God. The battle described in Ezekiel 39 may be a description of Armageddon in the months before the return of Christ. If so then Gog and Magog may be taken to symbolise once more the uniting of all nations against God and His people. Many have speculated that these names may refer to Russia. What is certain is that the Bible indicates here that all nations from the four corners of the earth will be involved, and that the number of combatants will be huge "as the sand of the sea."

The rebellion will be short lived and will be terminated not by conventional fighting and warfare, but by an act of God pouring fire from heaven. Then the devil will be cast into hell where he will be tormented forever and ever.

The Last Judgment

[11] I saw a great white throne, and him who sat on it, from whose face the earth and the heaven fled away. There was found no place for them. [12] I saw the dead, the great and the small, standing before the throne, and they opened books. Another book was opened, which is the book of life. The dead were judged out of the things which were written in the books, according to their works. [13] The sea gave up the dead who were in it. Death and Hades gave up the dead who were in them. They were judged, each one according to his works. [14] Death and Hades were thrown into the lake of fire. This is the second death, the lake of fire. [15] If anyone was not found written in the book of life, he was cast into the lake of fire.

John now saw Christ seated on a large white throne that has not been mentioned before in the Bible. Earth and heaven fled away and disappeared for ever. Peter prophesied this destruction of planet earth at the end of the age:

"But the day of the Lord will come as a thief in the night; in *which the heavens will pass away with a great noise, and the elements will be dissolved with fervent heat, and the earth and the works that are in it will be burned up." (2 Peter 3:10)*

His prophecy combines the second coming with the disappearance of heaven and earth. The Bible frequently skips over long periods of time in a single sentence. For example Joel saw the outpouring of the Holy Spirit at Pentecost and united it with the great and terrible day of the Lord, the Day of Judgment:

"It will happen afterward, that I will pour out my Spirit on all flesh;
and your sons and your daughters will prophesy.
Your old men will dream dreams.
Your young men will see visions.
[29] *And also on the servants and on the handmaids in those days, I will pour out my Spirit.*
[30] *I will show wonders in the heavens and in the earth: blood, fire, and pillars of smoke.*
[31] *The sun will be turned into darkness, and the moon into blood, before the great and terrible day of Yahweh comes.."*
(Joel 2:28-31)

The second resurrection will take place and the whole human race will be gathered before God. The believers will be present having already stood before Christ and given an account to Him immediately after their death.

Multitudes will stand before God and the books will be opened describing the works done by each person. The Bible consistently teaches that no-one will ever be saved by works, only by faith in Christ. However the Bible also teaches that though salvation is by faith, judgment will be according to our works. This means that living faith must alter a person's conduct or it is vain. James emphasised this aspect of salvation:

> *"Even so faith, if it has no works, is dead in itself. [18] Yes, a man will say, "You have faith, and I have works." Show me your faith without works, and I by my works will show you my faith.*
> *[19] You believe that God is one. You do well. The demons also believe, and shudder. [20] But do you want to know, vain man, that faith apart from works is dead?" (James 2:17-20)*

People will be judged by what is recorded in the books, which contain the deeds we have committed. The Book of Life is the most important one, containing the names of all who have trusted in Christ. This is the moment of the final separation of the human race between those who will spend eternity with God in the New Creation and those who will perish in the lake of fire, which is hell or the second death and eternal separation from God.

John also saw that death itself and hades were thrown into the lake of fire. This personification of death is puzzling and is not explained. Are there two angels called death and hades? Or perhaps this may simply refer to the fact that death and hades are abolished forever and will never be seen or mentioned again.

The Bible gives very limited information about what hell will be like. The most fearful description is in the fourteenth chapter of Revelation:

> *"He also will drink of the wine of the wrath of God, which is prepared unmixed in the cup of his anger. He will be tormented with fire and sulfur in the presence of the holy angels, and in the presence of the Lamb. [11] The smoke of their torment goes up forever and ever. They have no rest day and night, those who worship the beast and his image, and whoever receives the mark of his name." (Revelation 14:10-11)*

These verses indicate an eternity of torment without rest day or night for ever and ever. This verse does not suggest annihilation nor the hope of repentance and ultimate salvation for those in hell. The simple fact of eternal torment is disturbing but cannot be removed from the Bible. Every reader will long for more information but one can only conclude that we will only fully understand once we have entered into eternity and begin to understand the nature of time.

The doctrine of Annihilation Removes the Fear of God

The teaching that souls are not eternal and will be destroyed in hell contradicts the plain meaning of Revelation 14:10-11. Moreover if there is no hell after judgment day then sinners who say "Let us eat and drink, for tomorrow we die!" (Isaiah 22:13) are right to think they can enjoy the flesh and simply escape the consequences of their actions. Many sinners choose death rather than life believing they will be no more. The preaching of annihilation undermines the fear of death and judgment, since these will just be brief moments of transition before oblivion. If sinners are annihilated in hell then wicked men like Hitler and Stalin will have escaped lightly from a life of evil. If there is no hell, merely annihilation, then euthanasia and even suicide become attractive options to some.

Conclusion

Chapter 20 concludes the great convulsive conflicts between good and evil. God will triumph over all the powers of darkness and re-establish eternal foundations of righteousness. The victory over evil concludes with a final definitive separation of the human race between those who have chosen a life of sin and those who have chosen to love and serve God and His righteous ways.

CHAPTER 21

ALL THINGS NEW

The New Creation

Revelation 21:1 *I saw a new heaven and a new earth: for the first heaven and the first earth have passed away, and the sea is no more. [2] I saw the holy city, New Jerusalem, coming down out of heaven from God, prepared like a bride adorned for her husband. [3] I heard a loud voice out of heaven saying, "Behold, God's dwelling is with people, and he will dwell with them, and they will be his people, and God himself will be with them as their God. [4] He will wipe away from them every tear from their eyes. Death will be no more; neither will there be mourning, nor crying, nor pain, any more. The first things have passed away."*
[5] He who sits on the throne said, "Behold, I am making all things new." He said, "Write, for these words of God are faithful and true."

The last 2 chapters of the Bible mirror the first 2 chapters in Genesis in that the first Creation is replaced by the New Creation. There are of course huge contrasts indicating that this is not a mere restoration of the condition of things before the fall, but a progression. God has made something better in the New Creation. Here are some of the contrasts:

First Creation	New Creation
Seas and oceans	No sea
Day and Night	No night
Sun and Moon	No need of the sun or moon

Divisions will be abolished. There will no oceans separating people, and there will be no darkness either physical or spiritual. It can be also concluded that there will be no barrier between heaven and earth because God Himself is living in this new Creation.

The first creation began with the physical universe followed by the creation of humanity to inhabit it. The second creation began with the redemption of humanity at the cross. Redeemed humanity will pass over into the new creation. There is no creation of any being - not animal, human or angelic, in these two final chapters of Revelation.

From the final three chapters one can draw up a wonderful list of things that will be absent:

1. No sea: Rev 21:1
2. No more death: Rev 21:4
3. No sorrow: Rev 21:4
4. No crying: Rev 21:4
5. No more pain: Rev 21:4
6. No temple: Rev 21:22 (No religious structures)
7. No sun or moon: Rev 21:23
8. No sinners: Rev 21:27
9. No more curse: Rev 22:3
10. No more night: Rev 22:5
11. No devil or demons: Rev 20:10

This chapter makes declarations which will inspire all believers with the hope of a perfect world. Here are the main features of the New Creation revealed in this passage:

- The New Jerusalem is the bride and the title of the new humanity that will inhabit the new earth.

- God will live upon the earth among His people. God walked with Adam in the Garden of Eden and came down to live among the people of Israel in the tabernacle. God's desire has always been to live among His precious children.
- God will begin the era of the New Creation by wiping away all the tears from the eyes of His beloved people. There will evidently be a significant interval of strong emotions. There will be relief that the conflict is over. Many will have sorrow that some loved ones have chosen another path and are not there to share the joy. There will be the healing of wounds suffered during intense persecution. Whatever the cause of the weeping, God will minister comfort to His people, and sorrow and mourning shall cease forever.
- God will make all things new. There will be a regeneration of all things (Matthew 19:28) and a fresh new beginning. The mark of the new world will be that there will be no more sorrow or pain.

The Promise and the Warning

[6] He said to me, "It is done! I am the Alpha and the Omega, the Beginning and the End. I will give freely to him who is thirsty from the spring of the water of life. [7] He who overcomes, I will give him these things. I will be his God, and he will be my son. [8] But for the cowardly, unbelieving, sinners, abominable, murderers, sexually immoral, sorcerers, idolaters, and all liars, their part is in the lake that burns with fire and sulfur, which is the second death."

John then heard the renewed promise of the gospel ringing out not to the inhabitants of the New Creation, but to the readers of the book of Revelation. A time is coming when the door will be shut, but the book of Revelation is sent into the world so that all who hear may drink of the water of life and be saved. God will make them His children by the washing of New Birth. Whoever hears may experience the power of God to create a new heart, grant us a new beginning and so assure us of our place in that wonderful new world.

The magnificence of the promise is set against the solemnity of the warning. For those who reject God and His ways there will remain eternal separation from God with all the pain and torment of hell.

The New Jerusalem: The Lamb's Bride

[9] One of the seven angels who had the seven bowls, who were loaded with the seven last plagues came, and he spoke with me, saying, "Come here. I will show you the wife, the Lamb's bride." [10] He carried me away in the Spirit to a great and high mountain, and showed me the holy city, Jerusalem, coming down out of heaven from God, [11] having the glory of God. Her light was like a most precious stone, as if it were a jasper stone, clear as crystal; [12] having a great and high wall; having twelve gates, and at the gates twelve angels; and names written on them, which are the names of the twelve tribes of the children of Israel. [13] On the east were three gates; and on the north three gates; and on the south three gates; and on the west three gates. [14] The wall of the city had twelve foundations, and on them twelve names of the twelve Apostles of the Lamb. [15] He who spoke with me had for a measure, a golden reed, to measure the city, its gates, and its walls. [16] The city is square, and its length is as great as its width. He measured the city with the reed, twelve thousand twelve stadia (one thousand four hundred miles). Its length, width, and height are equal. [17] Its wall is one hundred forty-four cubits (two hundred and 16 feet or about sixty five meters), by the measure of a man, that is, of an angel. [18] The construction of its wall was jasper. The city was pure gold, like pure glass. [19] The foundations of the city's wall were adorned with all kinds of precious stones. The first foundation was jasper; the second, sapphire; the third, chalcedony; the fourth, emerald; [20] the fifth, sardonyx; the sixth, sardius; the seventh, chrysolite; the eighth, beryl; the ninth, topaz; the tenth, chrysoprasus; the eleventh, jacinth; and the twelfth, amethyst. [21] The twelve gates were twelve pearls. Each one of the gates was made of one pearl. The street of the city was pure gold, like transparent glass. [22] I saw no temple

in it, for the Lord God, the Almighty, and the Lamb, are its temple. [23] The city has no need for the sun, neither of the moon, to shine, for the very glory of God illuminated it, and its lamp is the Lamb. [24] The nations will walk in its light. The kings of the earth bring the glory and honor of the nations into it. [25] Its gates will in no way be shut by day (for there will be no night there), [26] and they shall bring the glory and the honor of the nations into it so that they may enter. [27] There will in no way enter into it anything profane, or one who causes an abomination or a lie, but only those who are written in the Lamb's book of life.

Then John was taken to a great high mountain where he saw the Bride the New Jerusalem in all its glory. Here are her characteristics:

- Clothed in glory, the brightness that emanates from God within her.
- 12 gates open day and night. There are no dangers or enemies here requiring barred gates.
- 12 angels at the gates. These magnificent beings will be visible and interact with human beings.
- 12 foundations named after the apostles. The promise of eternal holiness is founded on something God accomplished in His redemptive act and carried on in eternity. The ministers of God laid the foundations of this city through their ministry in the present gospel age.
- The foundations will be adorned with priceless shimmering precious gemstones. Paul refers to this in 1 Corinthians 3:12-15 where he taught that some things that are wrought in this present life will last forever. Some things will not survive the fire and be burnt up. He exhorts believers to allow the cross to work solid Christ like qualities that will endure forever, and warns believers not to pursue superficial and self-centred blessings.
- The city will be 1,500 miles square, in length, breadth and height. Some have speculated that this may be a cube, which would be hard to imagine. Perhaps only the highest point of the

city may be equal to its length and breadth. If so the city will reach upwards like a great mountain.
- The walls will be 72 metres high (144 cubits) – the equivalent of a 24 story building.
- It will be made of gold, as clear as glass. The gold is a symbol of the precious and beautiful quality of the inhabitants, infused with the divine nature. Gold covered the Ark of the Covenant (Exodus 25:11) and the interior walls of the Holy of Holies in Solomon's temple (1 Kings 6:20-22).
- The nations of those who are saved walk in the light of her. This is another description of the origins of the people who make up the New Jerusalem. They are no longer Jew nor Greek, but they have been saved from every kindred, tribe and tongue to partake of this unspeakable glory.
- There is no temple in the New Jerusalem. God is the temple and He is the light and the inner energy and life of everything. God will be all in all (1 Corinthians 15:28). The gospel never presents sinners with the option of heaven or hell, but rather with the option of Christ or sin. This is because all want to live in paradise, but not all love God who is the power and the brightness of paradise.

This Bride is a vast international city of people in love with Jesus, beautiful, holy, redeemed people, living in light, life and love. It is these people who are the glory and honour of the nations.

CHAPTER 22

THE SPIRIT AND THE BRIDE SAY COME

The Final Appeal

The River of Life

Revelation 22:1 *He showed me a river of water of life, clear as crystal, proceeding out of the throne of God and of the Lamb, ² in the middle of its street. On this side of the river and on that was the tree of life, bearing twelve kinds of fruits, yielding its fruit every month. The leaves of the tree were for the healing of the nations. ³ There will be no curse any more. The throne of God and of the Lamb will be in it, and his servants serve him. ⁴ They will see his face, and his name will be on their foreheads. ⁵ There will be no night, and they need no lamp light; for the Lord God will illuminate them. They will reign forever and ever.*

John now saw the river of life, the Holy Spirit, flowing from the throne. If an engineer saw this sight he would automatically look behind the throne to see where this vast river was coming from. This is because in nature there must be a cause and effect to all things. Something cannot flow from nothing. But God has no cause. He is Himself the source of all things. No matter how great the flow, God is never diminished, nor does He grow weak or weary. God is self-renewing and inexhaustible.

The river of life is clear and pure and makes all things live wherever it flows. This is no ordinary river for in the midst of its flow and on either side there are trees of life, bearing twelve kinds of fruit and giving a harvest all year round. The leaves themselves will have nourishing and healing properties. One could think that the word healing here implies that there will be sickness that needs treatment. Certainly all the wounds and scars of our former life will be swiftly healed forever in that life giving atmosphere. More than that, the leaves will be for the "healthing" of the nations, the imparting of positive health and well-being. Just as nourishment imparts health, so too the leaves of the tree will bestow wholeness to all.

The tree of life was in the Garden of Eden and the way to it was barred after the fall. Now the way is open and all may eat of its fruit. The tree of life was placed within the reach of every sinner when Christ died on the cross and poured out His life as an offering for sin. All who go to the cross and partake of His flesh and blood are eating of the tree of life. In the New Creation the tree of life will be available once more but this time without a cross of wood, without nails and a crown of thorns. Believers will feast at God's table in paradise.

The effects of the fall will be reversed and the curses spoken over creation at the fall of man will be lifted forever. All these blessings are because of the cross where Christ became a curse to remove this burden from the human race (Galatians 3:13). The power of the cross will have its full outworking in the New Creation because Jesus Christ broke the power of evil there and laid a new foundation of eternal righteousness in all who believe in Him.

Believers shall see God face to face. In the gospel of John the key word is "to believe." In John's epistles the key word is "to know." In the Revelation the key word is "to see." Believing turns to inner knowledge. Then in the New Creation we shall see with our eyes all that we believed. The sight of God's face will be the sweetest and most awesome moment of our existence. In that face is God's holiness and love bathed in depths of pulsating life. We shall look and look and be forced to cover our faces at the brightness of inexpressible and unapproachable glory. We shall know as we are known but there shall always be riches of personality and beauty that are beyond our gaze.

> *"Out of Zion, the perfection of beauty, God will shine forth."*
> *(Psalm 50:2 NKJV)*

The depths of the Godhead are not like any three dimensional sight we have ever seen. To gaze on God is to gaze on an infinity of transcendent beauty. As we behold God in His unveiled splendor, the riches of His tranquility of being, the heights of His love and the power of His holiness will be poured into our being. Believers already have access to this place by faith and many have experienced a foretaste of this bliss in rare moments of prayer, when the soul has taken flight and soared into the presence of God. Here we have but glimpses, but then we shall have the fullness of knowing God as we are known.

Night will have passed away, eternal day will have come and as God shares His being with His beloved children, so He will share His authority and they shall reign with Him.

The Time Is Near

[6] He said to me, "These words are faithful and true. The Lord God of the spirits of the prophets sent his angel to show to his bondservants the things which must happen soon."
[7] "Behold, I come quickly. Blessed is he who keeps the words of the prophecy of this book."
[8] Now I, John, am the one who heard and saw these things. When I heard and saw, I fell down to worship before the feet of the angel who had shown me these things. [9] He said to me, "See you don't do it! I am a fellow bondservant with you and with your brothers, the prophets, and with those who keep the words of this book. Worship God." [10] He said to me, "Don't seal up the words of the prophecy of this book, for the time is

at hand. *[11]{.sup} He who acts unjustly, let him act unjustly still. He who is filthy, let him be filthy still. He who is righteous, let him do righteousness still. He who is holy, let him be holy still."*

Once again John was stopped as he was about to prostrate himself in worship before the sublime being that was talking with him. John hears the astonishing words that this is none other than one of his fellow prophets, now glorified in heaven. The Bible is teaching us that when we pass into the wonderful realm of heaven after death, we will be transformed beyond our ability to comprehend.

John was commanded not to seal the words of Revelation because they were immediately relevant in John's day and will continue to be through every succeeding generation till the Lord returns. John's fellow prophet standing in the brightness of eternal glory told the readers that the time is near when choices will be fixed forever. Those who have chosen holiness will be holy eternally, and those who have chosen darkness will be eternally in the power of sin.

Jesus' Final Exhortation to His Own

[12] "Behold, I come quickly. My reward is with me, to repay to each man according to his work. [13] I am the Alpha and the Omega, the First and the Last, the Beginning and the End. [14] Blessed are those who do his commandments, that they may have the right to the tree of life, and may enter in by the gates into the city. [15] Outside are the dogs, the sorcerers, the sexually immoral, the murderers, the idolaters, and everyone who loves and practices falsehood. [16] I, Jesus, have sent my angel to testify these things to you for the assemblies. I am the root and the offspring of David; the Bright and Morning Star."
[17] The Spirit and the bride say, "Come!" He who hears, let him say, "Come!" He who is thirsty, let him come. He who desires, let him take the water of life freely.

Chapter Twenty-Two

Jesus now spoke a word of exhortation to His people. He pointed believers to the future hope when He will reward His faithful ones and grant them everlasting access to the tree of life. There is also another warning that immoral people will be excluded from the kingdom. All who inherit the kingdom of God were once sinners but they have forsaken the path of darkness and received the life transforming light of God's presence. This statement about sinners might be wrongly interpreted to suggest they might be in the New Creation but outside the city. This cannot be the case, since the great separation between the righteous and the unrighteous is the great gulf between the lake of fire and the new heaven and earth.

This section repeats three titles of Jesus:

1. *"Alpha and the Omega, the Beginning and the End, the First and the Last"*. This is the title by which Jesus was introduced in Revelation 1:8 and 11. It encompasses the book because it communicates the truth that the beginning of all things is in His hands as well as the end of all things. Jesus will have the first word and He alone will have the last word on every situation and every human being. There is great comfort in this knowledge, as we realise that nothing is finished till He has spoken and pronounced His loving, righteous and perfect wisdom.
2. *"The Root and the Offspring of David."* This title reminds the reader that Jesus Christ was grafted into the human race and is not ashamed to call us His brothers and sisters (Hebrews 2:11). Christ is wedded to humanity by His great love. He died for sinners so He might be joined with them forever in glory.
3. *"The Bright and Morning Star."* The morning star is the sun rising to bring warmth, light and life to the earth. Christ will be the light of the New Creation and there will be no more need of the sun and moon. There will be no more night in that perfect world.

The final exhortation of this section is an invitation for anyone who is thirsty to come and drink of the water of life. The Holy Spirit and the church (the Bride) are calling out across the world for whoever hears to come. He appeals to the hearer to also speak and say to themselves "Come!" This indicates that as God pleads and reasons with us, there must also come a moment when we agree with God and plead and reason with ourselves. We must believe and embrace the life changing promises of God.

A Final Solemn Warning

[18] I testify to everyone who hears the words of the prophecy of this book, if anyone adds to them, may God add to him the plagues which are written in this book. [19] If anyone takes away from the words of the book of this prophecy, may God take away his part from the tree of life, and out of the holy city, which are written in this book.

At the beginning of Revelation John had affirmed that whoever reads this book and whoever hears its words will be blessed. Now Jesus gave John a most solemn warning that is doubtless applicable to the whole Bible, but was spoken in particular reference to "the book of this prophecy." Jesus warned that this book must not be tampered with but must be held in reverence and awe. The penalty for altering this book will be to be blotted out of the book of life and suffer the plagues and torments prophesied in it.

I Come Quickly!

[20] He who testifies these things says, "Yes, I come quickly." Amen! Yes, come, Lord Jesus. [21] The grace of the Lord Jesus Christ be with all the saints. Amen.

In these final verses Jesus told John that He is coming quickly. This does not mean "soon" but "suddenly." John finally commends His readers to the grace of God. The age of gospel grace is drawing swiftly to its close,

Chapter Twenty-Two

and then all things that people have chosen in this world will be made permanent. Those who have chosen sin and darkness will find that that choice is now fixed for ever. There will be no more opportunity to repent. The day of final separation will soon be dawning. Let all who read make their eternal choice.

Study Guide

Clearing Our Minds

1. What is the mystery of the book of Revelation?
2. What do you think was the main purpose for which it was given?
3. Can you think of any events described in Revelation that match events in history? Why do you think this is so hard?
4. What are the main pitfalls to avoid? Why do you think so many commentators become fascinated with the sensational and dramatic aspects of the book?
5. Do you think the book is intended to point us to recognise events in the last days or simply to make sure we are ready for the Lord's return?
6. Think about all the believers who have lived and died over the past 2000 years. Was Revelation written for all generations or just for the last one?
7. Do you agree that the book is a call to worship?

Revelation 1

1. What is the significance of the fact that John was suffering for his faith along with other believers?
2. Pick out three aspects of the risen Christ that particularly speak to you.
3. Why do you think that the effect on John was to make him fall at Jesus feet as dead?
4. Can you see parallels between Jesus and Aaron trimming the oil lamps of the Holy Places?
5. Do you think this is this the most important chapter of the whole book? Give reasons for your answer.

Study Guide

Revelation 2

1. What is the meaning of the number seven? Are there any indications that it is not always to be taken literally?
2. Describe the positive qualities of the church at Ephesus.
3. How is this compatible with the main problem in the church? What does it mean to forsake one's first love? What steps can be taken to recover it?
4. Can you think of a nation which is suffering like the believers in Smyrna?
5. What is the most encouraging thing Jesus said to them?
6. What conclusions do you draw from the fact that Satan had a throne in Pergamos?
7. What was the main problem in Pergamos?
8. What does the Lord say to the church in Thyatira that makes you think their situation was even worse than Pergamos?

Revelation 3

1. What might be the marks of a church that has a name indicating life but is spiritually dead?
2. What was the main positive characteristic of the church in Philadelphia?
3. Discuss the name Philadelphia. Are we right to infer from the name that the church was full of love? Are there other indications that this was the case?
4. What was the problem in Laodicea? Why do you think this is a particularly difficult condition?
5. What was the advice of Jesus to the church?
6. What did He mean by telling them to "buy" from Him?

Revelation 4

1. What do you think it means to be "in the Spirit?"
2. What is the significance of the rainbow?
3. What does it mean that John saw 7 spirits of God?
4. Where does it give a similar description of heaven in the Bible?
5. Who do you think the 24 elders are?
6. What is the reason for their song of worship?

Revelation 5

1. Why did John weep so strongly?
2. What would have been the result if no one had been found worthy to open the scroll?
3. What is the reason for the new song of worship in this chapter? Do you think this was the first time it was sung?
4. What light does this chapter throw upon the cross?
5. Do you think God would have allowed the human race to live on without the coming of Christ to redeem the world? When might God have stopped human history if there were no Saviour?

Revelation 6

1. Reflect on the difference between our interpretation of a symbol and the truth we are teaching through it. Does it matter that much if we get our interpretation wrong? Is this inevitable given the mystery of the book? Is the challenge the key thing?
2. Write down what you think is the meaning of:
   a. The white horse
   b. The red horse
   c. The black horse
   d. The pale horse

   (You don't have to agree with the author's interpretation. Give your reasons for each answer).
3. The fifth seal opens a wave of persecution. What do you know about the persecuted church today and in history? Share some things you have read or know.
4. Why is it that all these seals are part of the power of redemption released through the blood of Jesus?
5. What is the significance behind the sixth seal? Do you agree that this refers to cosmic disturbances that have not yet taken place?

Study Guide

Revelation 7

1. What does it mean that believers are sealed?
2. This chapter seems to indicate a great number of believers both from Israel and the nations. Think of ways in which the Bible distinguishes between Jews and Gentiles. Are there contexts in which it is wrong to distinguish between these groups.
3. Read again the verses quoted from Romans. Do you agree that they seem to indicate a revival among the Jews leading to exciting, powerful repercussions among the nations?
4. What is unusual about the list of tribes? Write an explanation for the exclusion of Dan and Ephraim and the inclusion of Joseph and Manasseh.
5. Do you think that believers will pass through tribulation? Is that the obvious conclusion from these chapters? Could it refer to multitudes who have suffered greatly over the past centuries?
6. What are God's promises to those in tribulation?

Revelation 8

1. How is it possible that the prayers of God's people are answered by these judgments?
2. Can you see any indications from recent climate changes that could lead to the disasters described in this chapter?
3. What is the difference between tribulation and judgments poured out on the earth? Read Revelation 7:1-3 again. How do you think believers might be spared?
4. What do you conclude from the fact that "Chernobyl" means "wormwood?"
5. What does this chapter teach us about all natural disasters? Is it possible to hear the voice of God through these events?

Revelation 9

1. The release of a plague of demonic powers is scary to say the least. How might this be manifested?
2. Further demons are released from the river Euphrates and call the nations to war. What does this tell us about all wars? Does this teach us something about the weakness of human reason and institutions like the United Nations.

3. Do you think the description of an army in verses 17-19 could be the prophet John seeing a modern army through first century eyes?
4. What is the tragedy revealed in the last few verses? Do you think that the nations of the world were repentant after the Second World War?

Revelation 10

1. Reflect on the resplendent majesty of this angel and that he too worships Jesus the one who created all angels. What does this tell us about Christ?
2. Does the gospel age have a beginning and an end?
3. What is the little book? Why is Satan such an enemy of the little book?
4. Reflect on the history of the church and the significance of the rediscovery of the Bible in the Reformation.
5. What do you learn about the secrets of Bible reading?
6. What does this teach us about the only way the church can continue to have a prophetic ministry?

Revelation 11

1. Do you think from the overview given by the author that a 3rd temple will be built?
2. Do you agree that the mention of the temple here must be symbolical?
3. Do you think that the repeated prophecies about 42 months refer to a specific period of time at the end of the age?
4. What do you deduce from the previous fulfilments of this period of time in history e.g, the final solution of the Nazis in 1941?
5. What are the details of the description of the two witnesses that suggest two individuals?
6. What symbolical interpretation of the two witnesses is possible?
7. Why is the last trumpet and the coming of Christ described as the final woe?

Study Guide

Revelation 12

1. What does the woman teach us about God's plan throughout all the ages?
2. What is it that Satan so fiercely opposes?
3. Think of times when God took His people or His servants into the wilderness. What were the lessons that they learnt there?
4. In what way do we overcome Satan by the blood of the Lamb?
5. Why are the eagle's wings so essential for living a victorious Christian life?

Revelation 13

1. Describe the Antichrist in your own words.
2. Why do you think he will be so popular? Why will so many follow him?
3. Can you think of any other Antichrists in world history? What are the common threads?
4. Who or what is the false prophet? Think of the importance of the media in presenting governments to the public. Think of governments that control the media.
5. What is the significance of the number 666?
6. What is the meaning of the phrase "the Lamb slain from the foundation of the world?"

Revelation 14

1. Describe the believers referred to in heaven in your own words.
2. How do you imagine the angel will preach the gospel?
3. What are the elements of the gospel that are to be part of all gospel preaching?
4. What is the terrible fate awaiting those who worship the beast?
5. Compare the two reapings at the end of the age. What do they represent?

Revelation 15

1. The scene in heaven described in chapter 4 is repeated here. The difference is the multitudes. What are the attributes of God that they are singing about?

2. What is the song of Moses and the song of the Lamb? Think of the parallels between Exodus 15 and Revelation 15.
3. Why do you think the holy places were filled with smoke? Can you think of other times in the Bible when this happened?

Revelation 16

1. Do you agree with the author that these vials can be harmonised with the seven trumpets of chapter 8? What are the other occasions in the Bible when more than one account of the same event is given?
2. The sixth vial is the final war of Armageddon. What do you learn about the uncontrollable forces that bring the world to this war? Do you think the demonic powers could do this if human beings were not willing to be led in this way? What are the sins that lie behind wars?
3. The seventh vial represents the last trumpet and the return of Christ. What are the special details given in this chapter about His return?
4. What is the message to the heart from all these events?

Revelation 17

1. Write a line about what each of these Old Testament books teach us about Babylon:
    a. Genesis
    b. Isaiah
    c. Daniel
2. What are the qualities of Babylon that demonstrate she is the opposite of the church?
3. What do the ten horns and the waters represent?
4. Many believers have wondered whether the European Union is the modern form of Babylon and the Roman Empire. What do you think?

Revelation 18

1. How might Babylon be destroyed in one day?
2. What does the sudden destruction tell you about the world in which we live in? Why do you think people and governments love big buildings and monuments?
3. Babylon trades in luxury commodities but also in the bodies and souls of men. What does this tell you about the hidden darkness behind the business and political empires of the world?
4. Do you think many people close their eyes to the darker side of capitalism and politics? What are these hidden works of darkness?
5. How can we obey the exhortation to come out of Babylon?

Revelation 19

1. Why will believers rejoice at the fall of Babylon?
2. War and a wedding. What must we do to be ready for the marriage supper? Read Matthew 22:11 and Matthew 25:1-13.
3. The coming of Christ will be with terrible conquering power. What are His qualities that strike terror into sinners?
4. Who are the armies from heaven riding on white horses?
5. The last battle of Armageddon will be terrible. What are the most fearful aspects of this battle?

Revelation 20

1. When will the millennium begin?
2. Why would God give humanity such an experience?
3. Many will still reject Christ in the millennium. What does this teach you about the human heart?
4. The last battle of all will be short lived. What does this last gasp of Satan teach about the kingdoms of light and darkness?
5. What will be the basis of the last judgment?
6. Unbelievers will be sent to hell. Why do you think this doctrine of hell is so attacked?

Revelation 21

1. Describe the differences between the old and the new creation.
2. From the list of 11 things that will be absent in the new creation is there anything that particularly impacts you? Is there anything that surprises you?
3. Contrast the promises and the warnings of this chapter. In what way does this affect our preaching of the gospel?
4. The description of the New Jerusalem is quite mind-blowing. Describe some of the aspects that are particularly hard to grasp. What do you conclude from this?

Revelation 22

1. What is the river of life? Why is it so baffling to human minds that such a flow can come from a throne?
2. What is the greatest bliss described in this chapter that fills you with most awe?
3. John is tempted to worship the angel in verse 8, but it is his fellow servant. What does this tell you about the future glory for all of God's people?
4. What are the positive exhortations of this chapter?
5. Describe the last solemn warnings of the book in your own words.

Appendix 1: The four main methods of interpreting Revelation.

There are four main methods of interpreting the Book of Revelation and other New Testament writings about the coming of Christ. These four methods are not always competing methods. They are simply four ways in which truth must be drawn from the book. In this way it can be seen that the book speaks on different levels to all the ages of the church from the first century to the last years immediately preceding the return of Christ.

I Preterist.

The Preterist view interprets the Book of Revelation and other passages such as Matt 24 as referring to events that took place in the first century AD. So the Abomination of Desolation occurred when the Roman armies desecrated and destroyed the Temple in AD 70. Many of the prophecies of Jesus unquestionably referred to events that were to take place within a short period of time. This included the crisis in Judea which led to the fall of Jerusalem. Jesus said that armies would surround Jerusalem: Luke 21:22-24. The siege and fall of Jerusalem were a period of terrible tribulation for the Jews, which could be the meaning of the prophecy in Matt 24:21. The Christians heeded the warnings of Jesus and fled from Judea to a town called Pella in modern day Jordan in AD 67. There were false Messiahs in the siege who claimed that God would deliver them. Jesus said that Jerusalem would fall and that it would be trodden underfoot till the time of the Gentiles was fulfilled.

However, Jesus also gave prophecies that were not fulfilled in the first century. For example, He said that the fig tree would blossom again: Matt 24:32. He said that the angels would gather His elect from the four corners of the compass: Matt 24:31. These are prophecies that relate to the end of the age, not merely to the first century. It is difficult to see how they have already been fulfilled in the first century.

It is also important to recognise the *cyclical* fulfilment of prophecy. By this is meant that there is more than one fulfilment of a prophecy. Take for example the prophecy of the *Abomination of Desolation*. This prophecy was originally given by Daniel: Daniel 8:11-13 and 11:31. It was fulfilled by the desecration of the temple in 167-164 BC by

Antiochus Epiphanes. But Jesus refers to it as something future, which was fulfilled in AD 70 but certainly has further fulfilments, including the misuse of papal authority in the Middle Ages, and the Muslim occupation of Jerusalem. The Dome of the Rock on the temple mount is also a fulfilment of this prophecy which continues to the present day. On the inside of the prayer area in the dome is an inscription stating that Mohammed is God's prophet and God has no Son. I John 2:22 states "He is Antichrist who denies the Father and the Son." There will probably still be a further fulfilment of this prophecy and of other prophecies. Jerusalem will yet again be surrounded by armies.

II. *Historical.*

The historical method of interpreting the prophecies of the New Testament is based on the belief that these prophecies are concerning the unfolding of events in the whole of the church age. According to this method, the seals of Revelation 6 are events in history. The Reformation is symbolised by the discovery of the little book in Revelation chapter 10 and by the death and resurrection of the two witnesses in Revelation chapter 11. This method of interpretation is fascinating and its proponents are convincing. But this method requires a vast knowledge of history which has only been available to few of the generations of Bible readers since the Bible was written. The breadth of information needed to develop this interpretation is not available to most readers in developing nations and so is irrelevant to such readers. This method of Bible interpretation has fewer proponents in the 20th and 21st centuries, but was quite popular in the 19th century. Whether or not the symbols of Revelation can be tied to specific events in world history, the Book of Revelation undeniably teaches the ways of God in history. Hence, we know that there are changes in the course of history, not merely because men have made a political decision, but rather because Christ opened a seal in heaven.

III. *Symbolical.*

This method interprets the Book of Revelation by looking at the imagery in other parts of the Bible. Thus when Babylon is mentioned, a study of the origins of this city reveals that it is the site where the tower of Babel was built. It is the city where Daniel was in exile for nearly the whole seventy years of the captivity. Babylon is the head of gold in Nebuchadnezzar's vision in Daniel chapter 2. Most of the symbols used in the Book of Revelation can be found in other parts of the Bible. This enables the reader to understand the processes of the end times and thus work out the meaning of the Book.

IV. Futurist.

The Futurist method is that which interprets the whole Book of Revelation as referring to a very short period of time at the end of history. There are many variations of this interpretation, some that believe in a pre-tribulation and some in a post-tribulation rapture.

The futurist interpretation taught by J.N. Darby and the Scofield Bible.

In 1830 a Scottish believer named Margaret Macdonald received a prophetic revelation that Christians would be taken up to heaven in the rapture before the Great Tribulation. J.N. Darby embraced this teaching and through his extensive ministry and authority this interpretation quickly became popular. He taught in America and a Bible teacher named Cyrus Scofield embraced Darby's dispensationalism and his interpretation of the book of Revelation. He incorporated Darby's views into his study bible. It is through these steps that Darby's interpretation has been adopted by many denominations and Bible colleges throughout the world.

Darby's central emphasis was to interpret Revelation chapter 4:1-2 as a description of the rapture of the church, and not merely the moment that John was caught up to heaven in a vision. Darby's main argument for this is the absence of the word "church" from the end of the third chapter of Revelation onwards. But John describes many scenes in heaven where the redeemed worship (Revelation 15:1-3) but the word "church" is not used either to describe people in heaven or on earth. The word "church" is also absent from the entire book of Romans except the last chapter 16. It only occurs once in Hebrews (Hebrews 12:23) where it refers to the church in heaven not on earth. The Bible uses different words to describe the same thing. For example, the word disciple appears nowhere in the New Testament after the book of Acts. But it would be wrong to conclude that the writers of the epistles disagreed with Jesus command to go and make disciples of all nations. In fact the epistles are aimed at fulfilling that command. The saints who overcome the beast in Revelation 12 are surely members of Christ's body the church (Revelation 12:11).

Which is the right method?

While I respect these four views it is nevertheless right that I make it clear which one I believe to be the most accurate. I have adopted the symbolical method because in my view it is the one that is founded on the self-interpretation of Bible symbols. By this I mean that the Bible student on every continent and in every age has the same Bible at his or her disposal. One can therefore interpret the frequent references to Old Testament individuals such as Balaam and Jezebel. One is able to connect the two witnesses with Moses and Elijah because they also shut up heaven that rain should not fall and turned water to blood (Revelation 11:6; Exodus 7:14-24 and 1 Kings 17:1). We are also able to understand the meaning of Babylon by studying references to Babel (Hebrew for Babylon, Genesis 11) and the experiences of the exiles in the Babylonian captivity (Isaiah 14, Daniel 2, and Jeremiah 51 to name but a few Old Testament references to Babylon).

While my main line of interpretation is symbolical, I nevertheless believe in the futurist interpretation because this prophecy concerns major future events. Revelation culminates in real events such as the battle of Armageddon. A symbolical approach should confirm and strengthen the belief in a sudden real return of the Lord at the climax of human history.

I am however uncomfortable with the Scofield Bible and Darby's interpretation of the end times. A few interpreters have concluded that the book of Revelation is mainly written for those who are left behind after a secret rapture. I believe the rapture of the saints will take place after the tribulation at the return of Christ to rule the world.

Conclusion: gleaning understanding from all 4 views

It is certain that some of the prophecies refer to the first century. The Book of Revelation also teaches principles of history that can and must be applied to the whole two thousand years of church history. There is also no controversy that the Book of Revelation must be interpreted in the light of symbols and illustrations in the Old Testament scriptures. Moreover the fact that the book reveals the future is also beyond doubt.

The only conclusion that can be reached is that the Book speaks to us on several different levels and that we must seek to draw understanding from all four of these methods of studying the Book. The Book of Revelation throws light on human history. However there are some views of the Book of Revelation that are very tenuous. These tend to be based on current affairs. John Wesley was convinced that the Turkish Ottoman Empire was the Antichrist kingdom. Believers during the cold war believed that the USSR was the Antichrist. Such views are interesting and have some contribution to make but are often proved wrong by the flow of history.

Appendix 2: Four lists of the twelve tribes.

The twelve tribes listed in Revelation 7 are an unusual selection. There were twelve sons of Jacob making the twelve original tribes. Then the tribe of Joseph was replaced by Joseph's two sons Ephraim and Manasseh. This produced 13 tribes, but only 12 inherited land in Joshua's day because Levi was set aside to minister among all the twelve tribes.

There are four significant occasions when the 12 tribes of Israel are listed and each time the list is different.

Genesis 49	Joshua 13-21	Ezekiel 48	Revelation 7
Reuben	Reuben	Reuben	Reuben
Simeon	Simeon	Simeon	Simeon
Judah	Judah	Judah	Judah
Gad	Gad	Gad	Gad
Asher	Asher	Asher	Asher
Naphtali	Napthali	Naphtali	Naphtali
Issachar	Issachar	Issachar	Issachar
Benjamin	Benjamin	Benjamin	Benjamin
Zebulon	Zebulon	Zebulon	Zebulon
Levi	Levi	-	Levi
Dan	Dan	Dan	-
Joseph	-	-	Joseph
-	Manasseh	Manasseh	Manasseh
-	Ephraim	Ephraim	-
12 tribes	13 tribes	12 tribes	12 tribes

1. The list in Genesis 49 is of the original 12 sons of Jacob.
2. The list In Joshua 13 to 21 refers to the division of the land for all 13 tribes.
3. The list in Ezekiel 48 is the same as that of Old Testament Israel inheriting the land under Joshua with the exception of Levi. This may be because Levi was to inherit cities among all the tribes as in Joshua 21.
4. Revelation 7 has produced a unique list excluding Ephraim and Dan and including Joseph and Levi. The exclusion of Dan may be because his name means "judge" and in heaven judgment has passed. Manasseh is included and means "forgetting" and in

heaven all the woes and pains of earth are forgotten forever. Ephraim means "fruitful" but is replaced with Joseph. The name Ephraim was used in the Old Testament as a synonym for the northern kingdom. For this reason Ephraim was representative of the worst corruption of the 10 tribes.

"Ephraim will become a desolation in the day of rebuke. Among the tribes of Israel, I have made known that which will surely be.." (Hosea 5:9)

Joseph on the other hand has the beauty and fragrance of a beautiful life full of forgiveness and grace.

The choice of the twelve tribes confirms the symbolic nature of this list. It would be extraordinary if none from the tribes of Dan and Ephraim was saved on the final day. So the list symbolises all the elect from Israel redeemed and glorified in heaven.

Bibliography

Beale, G.K. and D.H. Campbell, *Revelation a shorter commentary,* Eerdmans Publishing 2015.

Bell, Bernard, *The Book of Revelation: the Seen and the Unseen,* 2001–2007 Peninsula Bible Church Cupertino

E.H. Broadbent, *The Pilgrim Church,* Pickering and Inglis London, 1931.

Gentry, Kenneth L. , Sam Hamstra, C. Marvin Pate and Robert L. Thomas. *Four Views on the Book of Revelation*, Zondervan 1998. Four authors explain their different views on Revelation.

Graham, Billy, *Approaching Hoof beats*, , Hodder and Stoughton 1983. A futurist view of the horsemen of the apocalypse.

Johnson, Dennis E. *The Triumph of the Lamb* P & R Publishing 2001

Ladd, George Eldon *A Commentary on the Book of Revelation*, , Eerdmans 1972. Ladd explains in his introduction that his is a blend of the historical and the futurist methods of interpretation

Parkyns, Edgar *His Waiting Bride*, Wheatcorn publications 1996. This is a walk through church history hand in hand with the book of Revelation.

Pawson, David *When Jesus Returns,* , Hodder and Stoughton 1995.

Poythress, Vern S. *The Returning King* Presbyterian and Reformed Publishing 2000

Sidlow Baxter, J. *Explore the Book,*. First published 1955. Republished by Zondervan 2010. A short introduction to the Book of Revelation by a moderate futurist, in this commentary on the whole Bible.

Sproul, R.C.. *The Last Days According to Jesus* Baker Books 1998. This is a thorough examination of the New Testament in the light of the preterist interpretation.

Index

Abaddon	77
Aids	58
Antichrist	111 ff.
Antiochus Epiphanes	116
Apollyon	77
Armageddon	72, 158
Asia	18
Babylon	137, 148
Balfour	109
Black Death	57
Boniface VIII	90
Bottomless Pit	76
Chesterton, G.K.	5, 98
Calvary	51
Chernobyl	73
Diognetus	31
Domitian	9, 10
Ephesus	20
Euphrates	72, 79, 135
European Union	145
Farrar, F.W.	25
French Revolution	54
Fukushima	73
Goebbels	118
Gog	162
Great Tribulation	67
Hell	126, 166
Hiroshima	54
Hitler	3, 94, 117
Jezebel	33
Kells, Book of	48
Lampstand	24
Laodicea	40
Lloyd George	109
Lord's day	10
Lucifer	139
Luther, Martin	3, 77
Mohammed	89
Menorah	24
Magog	162
Mao Tse Tung	54, 94
Millennium	159
Nagasaki	54
Nebuchadnezzar	140
Nee. Watchman	36
Nero	9, 116
Nicolaitans	25
Nimrod	137
Olivet discourse	60
Ottoman Empire	3
Pergamos	29
Pergamum Museum	30
Philadelphia	38
Polycarp	26
Popes	90
Rainbow	45
Ramsay, Sir William	29
Rapture	2
Rome	141
Rubens	48
Russian Revolution	54
Sardis	35
Shakespeare	56
Smyrna	26
Spanish flu	58
Spanish Inquisition	27
Stalin	94
Temple	88
Thyatira	32
Titus	89
Trajan	9
Tribes of Israel	64, 65, 193
Trieste martyrs	58
Tyndale, William	3
Wartburg	77
Wesley, John	3
Whitefield, George	85
Wigglesworth, Smith	86
Wormwood	73

Printed in Poland
by Amazon Fulfillment
Poland Sp. z o.o., Wrocław